The Adventure of Saying

YES

A Field Guide for Power Evangelism and a Life of Miracles

JonMark Baker

SUPERNATURAL TRUTH PRODUCTIONS, LLC
Practical Training for Spirit-Filled Living
www.SupernaturalTruth.com

ISBN: 978-0-9988171-6-3

Endorsements:

These days, everyone wants to be on a platform, but I have met very few people who are actually passionate about the Great Commission that Christ left for His followers. JonMark is the kind of person for whom it is absolutely normal to see miracles of healing outside the doors of the Church, as he frequently uses the gift of words of knowledge to minister to the lost. I thank God for his life and ministry, and I recommend his story. May we all take the message of Jesus outside the doors of the Church until the Lamb of God receives the full reward for His sufferings!

Lydia S. Marrow
Shake the Nations

JonMark takes the "spooky" out of spiritual in this compelling yet wonderfully approachable book. It is humble, honest, and even humorous. I couldn't stop reading! In masterfully weaving personal miracle stories with good theology and practical wisdom, JonMark encourages us all that we can truly know God and make Him known too."

Josh Adkins
Pastor, Loft Church, Herrin, IL

This book will take you on a journey into the heart of God. You'll discover His love for you and what His love looks like through you. JonMark will help equip you to live in the supernatural power of the Holy Spirit, to heal the sick, speak prophetic words, preach the Gospel, cast out demons, and show the eternal love of Christ to a world that desperately needs it."

Sean Smith
Evangelist
Author, I Am Your Sign
and Prophetic Evangelism

JonMark Baker has always impressed me. I've observed him in action for years in various events and venues. His book, The Adventure of Saying Yes, is, in my opinion, a "must-read" for every believer who really loves God and people. Get ready for a miracle adventure as you read. Each chapter keeps you riveted to God's love and shows how you can partner with Jesus in His miracle-working love.

Dave Williams
Bishop, Mount Hope Church, Lansing, MI
Apostolic Elder, Harvest Christian Churches
Author, The Art of Pacesetting Leadership

I have known JonMark Baker since he was a child and have watched him grow into an individual with a genuine passion for both God and people. He is equally passionate about seeing people encounter the Lord in supernatural ways. Since my own personal conversion occurred through a "power encounter" with Jesus, I am obviously glad to see this emphasis!

Jeff Hlavin
Superintendent
Assemblies of God, Michigan District

JonMark is a prophetic and apostolic leader in the Church. In his book, *The Adventure of Saying YES*, JonMark adroitly and pragmatically breaks down the challenges and fears so many Christians face when sharing their faith. From discerning the voice of the Holy Spirit and stepping out in faith for the miraculous to touch a person's life, JonMark addresses the pathway to efficacious ministry. His work is engaging through storyline, questions, and action steps to assist the reader in coming closer to Jesus and His will. *The Adventure of Saying YES* is an outstanding book for all followers of Jesus to read and study.

E. Scott Martin
National Director
Chi Alpha Campus Ministries

Acknowledgments

I would like to thank Art Thomas for his encouragement, guidance, time, and hard work in helping me produce this book. I never would have finished it were it not for you. Sincerely, thanks for everything.

I would like to thank my beautiful wife, Kara, for being such a huge encouragement to me. I couldn't have this adventure without you, nor would I want to.

Thanks to my parents, John and Bethany Baker, for celebrating my victories with me and encouraging me to continue pursuing God for the miraculous when I was discouraged and disappointed. Thanks for believing in me.

Thank You, God. This book is dedicated to You. These are Your stories, these are Your victories. Thank You for holding my hand and walking with me through discouragement and celebration. Thank You for forgiving my sins and empowering me to live righteously. Thank You for giving me Jesus and filling me with the Holy Spirit. Thank You for being my Father. I pray that this book glorifies You and encourages more of Your kids to walk with You in the adventures You have for them.

The Adventure of Saying YES – JonMark Baker

Table of Contents

Foreword

by Art Thomas

"I think the Lord told me to go into that adult bookstore and pray for somebody."

This is what it's like being friends with JonMark Baker—not the adult bookstores specifically, but having your plans diverted by the sudden and unexpected prompting of the Holy Spirit.

After sharing lunch together, I rode in a car with JonMark (a missionary to university students) and his dad (a seasoned pastor). That's when JonMark surprised us with his statement about the bookstore. His dad and I were hesitant. We were all in town together for a large gathering of ministers in Michigan, and the thought of our colleagues in ministry seeing us walking out of an adult bookstore didn't seem like the image any of us wanted to convey.

But not wanting to argue with the Holy Spirit, we reluctantly agreed. JonMark turned his car around and parked in front of the store.

So a pastor, a missionary, and an evangelist walked into an adult bookstore . . . and that wasn't the setup to a bad joke. This was real life!

The place was empty of people apart from the guy behind the counter.

"Can I help you find something?" asked the man, surrounded by products that might even make a non-minister blush.

"Actually," JonMark answered, "I felt like God wanted us to come here and offer to pray for you. Do you have back pain?"

The guy looked a little freaked out and didn't want to have anything to do with us.

"Nope. And you can all leave."

JonMark's dad and I were balancing disappointment with relief as JonMark said a few quick words about God's love for the guy and started toward the exit. We were relieved to be leaving that awkward situation. But we were also disappointed because we were leaving without an "awesome testimony" to alleviate the concerns of any pastors who might see us all coming out of the store.

Did the guy actually have back pain? Beats me (though it wouldn't surprise me at all if he did). It looked like we might have wasted our time and risked our reputations for nothing.

Immediately as we exited the store, a woman went limping past the front of our car.

"Excuse me! I see you're limping. What happened?"

The woman explained her severe pain and showed us the electronic TENS unit she was using to manage it. She had been in a car accident and had suffered greatly ever since.

Within five or ten minutes of ministry in Jesus' name, the woman miraculously regained her mobility and said she wasn't experiencing any more pain. Following the Holy Spirit's lead, JonMark shared a few details about the woman's life including bad dreams she had been having and a couple of other physical ailments. And with a simple gospel presentation, she prayed with us there in the parking lot. She had a history with the Lord but hadn't been to church in years. After this encounter, she wanted to start going again. Since none of us lived in the area, we gave her the information for the church where our meeting was being held and parted ways.

It's hard to talk about JonMark without making him sound like some sort of a superhero. It would be easy to hear a story like this and say, "Wow! That guy is a seriously gifted and powerful Christian!"

Well, he is.

But so are you. The stories you'll read in this book aren't meant to prop up JonMark as someone unique. They're meant to show you what "normal Christianity" looks like.

The book in your hands is an invitation into a lifestyle of saying yes to Jesus just like JonMark does. Experience tells me it's near impossible to spend much time with JonMark without being challenged to know Jesus more intimately and represent Him more effectively. I believe this book will do the same for you.

As you read, try to imagine JonMark's testimonies as though you're right there in the story. Put yourself in his shoes. See yourself doing the same things. I know JonMark didn't share any of these stories to make himself look amazing. Instead it's all to show you what is possible when someone like you loves and trusts Jesus enough to say yes. Every story in this book can be your story too as you spend time with the Lord and apply the principles shared.

It has been a joy to know JonMark for the last several years, and it has been an honor to call him my friend. I know few people who dedicate themselves to such a lifestyle of integrity, humility, and genuine love for Jesus and others. It is my privilege to recommend this book to you. May you encounter the Holy Spirit as you read and never be the same in Jesus' name.

Art Thomas
Missionary-Evangelist, Author, and Filmmaker
www.ArtThomas.org

Introduction

I'M SITTING AT A COFFEE SHOP. MOMENTS AGO, I WAS trying to think of what to write in this introduction. Just then, a woman walked in front of my table.

Instantly the Lord told me she has migraine headaches, a curve in her lower back that causes sciatica, pain in her stomach on the right side that she experiences about twice per day, nightmares, insomnia, and anxiety.

This woman is a member of the local Native American tribe and practices spiritual healing, but Jesus had her number. I prayed for her and shared the love of God. While I wasn't able to fully share the gospel with her, I was able to shake her presuppositions about Christianity and plant a seed that will prayerfully blossom into saving faith.

This is a typical day for me—not because I am special but because God is so much fun.

Have you ever read the Bible and thought, *Wow! I wish I could have adventures with God like Paul*?

You can!

God has not grown boring over the years. He is still doing great miracles and exploits through people who are willing to say yes to Him. God desires to use ordinary Christians like you and me in extraordinary ways.

The biblical adventures in the Book of Acts are just the beginning for those who will pay attention to the voice of God and yield to Him. In this book I share real adventures that God has taken me on. From healings in grocery stores to psychic shops to hospital rooms, God is always up to something.

As you read, you will learn to heal the sick, share prophetic words, cast out demons, share the gospel, and much more. The Holy Spirit is the most fun, adventurous Person in the universe. I want to teach you how to pay attention to His voice and yield to Him so that you can have adventures with Him beyond what you thought possible.

I pray that this book encourages you, inspires you, and helps you to walk with Jesus daily—to yield to Him in everything and glorify Him through the adventurous life He longs to lead you into. May my ceiling be your floor, and may these stories be just the beginning for you as you dare to step out into the impossible.

CHAPTER 1

He Loves Me, He Loves Me Not

Panic! My heart began to race, and adrenaline coursed through my body as I realized this was the end. The rapture had taken place, and I had missed it.

When I was nine, a popular fiction series was making its rounds through my church. It chronicled the adventures of a group of people who were left behind after the rapture but resisted the antichrist as they struggled to survive in a post-apocalyptic world. The story captured my young imagination. Then one day, as my parents left me at home to go to the grocery store, the thought occurred to me, *What if the rapture happened and I missed it?*

Images of me stockpiling food and ammunition, gathering a team of people, and finding a remote place to hunker down and weather the Great Tribulation began racing through my head. *How could I have missed it?! How could this happen?! What do I do?!*

And then my parents pulled into the driveway.

I began to catch my breath, but the thoughts never went away. I could never get away from the idea that I wasn't going to make it to heaven. My parents would be sleeping, and I would poke open the door just to make sure they were still there. Even into my upper teenage years, I could never be away from my parents without being seized by anxiety and panic.

The fear began to grow, and the thoughts that dominated my mind began to take other forms. *What if I'm the antichrist? What if I'm destined for hell? Is there any salvation for someone like me?*

I lived in an internal world without forgiveness, without hope, bound for hell. The panic attacks grew worse. I needed a savior, but I knew there wasn't one for me. My sin was too terrible. I had sinned far too grievously for God's forgiveness to work for me. I deserved hell, and no matter how hard I prayed or how long I wept, I knew there was no hope.

I might as well end it now. To go on living is to delay the inevitable. These were the kinds of thoughts that haunted me on a daily basis.

I would have moments where God would speak to my heart. Once I told God, "I don't know if You will ever love me, or if You even like me, but please, I need You right now."

"I will never turn away someone with a heart like yours," the Lord said. And then it was as if Jesus Himself were standing next to me. I felt relief for a time until the next thought came, and I went back into my tailspin.

This was my adolescence. I grew up the son of a pastor, knowing the Word of God better than most, but dominated by a lie that God could never forgive me. God's grace was never a reality to me. His love was something for others to enjoy—others who were much holier and more righteous than I. I never even felt like I belonged in church. *These people know God*, I thought. *I have no business with these people.* I felt utterly alone and was a slave to fear. I was a condemned person, destined for an eternity without God.

Fighting the Lie

Far too often Christians live their lives under various versions of this lie:

"You really blew it. You need to get your act together before God will ever accept you."

Or, "How dare you worship God on Sunday? You know what you did this week! What business do you have even coming to church? You have nothing in common with these holy people."

Or satan's personal favorite: "God loves everyone, but you are the exception."

In Scripture, the "father of lies" has always tried to make people question two things: God's character and their identity.

"Did God really say, 'You must not eat from any tree in the garden'?" This is the question satan asked of Eve in Genesis 3.

Of course that is not what God said. God said there was only one tree from which Adam and Eve were not to eat. However, satan was planting a seed of doubt. Eve responded to satan:

> "We may eat fruit from the trees in the garden, but God did say, 'You must not eat from the tree that is in the middle of the garden, and you must not touch it or you will die.'"
>
> "You will not surely die," the serpent said to the woman. "For God knows that when you eat of it your eyes will be opened, and you will be like God, knowing good and evil."
>
> *Genesis 3:2–5*

Here, the devil calls into question God's goodness. The enemy of our soul plants the idea that God is holding back something good from us. He paints the false picture of a threatened, envious god who would hold back something good from Adam and Eve so they don't become like Him.

In the temptation of Jesus, satan continually challenged Jesus' identity. Every time he said to Jesus, "If you are the Son of God . . . ," the devil tried to get Jesus to doubt His identity and act accordingly. If the devil can undermine your understanding of God's goodness and your identity, he can potentially thwart your destiny.

We must understand that everything we do is a manifestation of our identity. As Christians, our identities are directly influenced by our perception of God's character. With every action we take, we are answering the unspoken question, "Who do you think you are?"

If you view yourself as a shy person, you will manifest that perception of yourself in social situations. In every situation you encounter, your actions are dictated by your perception of your identity. Is it any wonder that satan would choose this as one of his primary targets?

In my life the two issues of God's goodness and my identity were the major targets of the lies of the devil. God was never going to forgive me, I thought, and I was unacceptable to Him.

But thank God there is One who reveals the truth. He is much more skilled at revealing truth than satan is at concealing it. He is the Holy Spirit, and I met Him one summer as a teen.

God's Love Changes Everything

I walked into the chapel at Lost Valley Bible Camp in Gaylord, Michigan. I had gone there for junior high and senior high camps and was mostly concerned with who I would flirt with at the snack shop after service. But this time when I walked into the chapel, I encountered something overwhelming. A wave of divine love washed over me. I felt the weighty glory of God settle on me, and at the age of fifteen I began to weep uncontrollably.

You need to understand, there was no band playing worship music. The first service of the week had not even begun. But there were humble people fasting and praying in that room all day long, and when I walked in I stepped into a wall of God's tangible presence. His love began to shatter the lies that I was unaccepted and un-forgiven. The Revealer of Truth began to whisper into my spirit that I am adopted into the family of God.

> The Spirit you received does not make you slaves, so that you live in fear again; rather, the Spirit you received brought about your adoption to sonship. And by Him we cry, "Abba, Father."
> *Romans 8:15*

In that moment, I told the Lord, "If You're really this good, I'll serve You for the rest of my life."

I was born again. I had always been a believer, but in that moment I was made alive inside. From then on I had a confidence that I belonged to God and that He belonged to me. Nothing held me back from the love of God. The lies of the devil were crushed under the weight of God's mercy and love.

The Power of Your Story

You may now be thinking, *Isn't this book about power evangelism?*

Yes, it is! And my story has everything to do with that. First, the love of God and the power of the gospel are the foundation of evangelism. If you have not first received this love, you have nothing to offer the world. Second, your testimony is the most powerful evangelistic tool you have in your tool belt. Your testimony is the gospel in action. When you share your testimony with someone, you are showing them what God can do for them too.

I remember one autumn evening when I was a senior in college. I was outside of my on-campus apartment, talking on the phone with my fiancée (now my beautiful wife, Kara). I was leading a campus ministry called Chi Alpha, and I was always looking for opportunities to share the gospel with people.

While still on the phone, I saw a guy sitting on the steps of the Arts Center. I immediately felt as though the Holy Spirit was leading me to go talk to him. I hung up the phone and went to speak with him.

"Hey, how's it going, man?" I asked as I approached.

"Good, how are you doing?" he replied with a curious look on his face. It was nighttime, and I was a stranger approaching him out of nowhere, so he was naturally on guard.

This guy's name was Tom, and he was the president of a fraternity on campus that was pretty well known for their parties.

"This may sound weird, but I am a Christian, and I felt like God wanted me to come pray for you. Is there anything I could pray for you about?"

"Not really, man. I'm doing fine."

"Is there any pain in your body or anything?" I asked, hoping for something.

"No, man. I'm doing fine."

Suddenly I felt the Holy Spirit directing me to share my testimony. I shared with him the story I just shared with you, but much more awkwardly.

"Cool, man," he said in response to my testimony. "Good for you."

That was that. I left, feeling a little stupid but grateful for having been obedient to the voice of God.

The next week I was in the library and suddenly felt a hand on my shoulder. I turned around, and it was Tom.

"Dude, thank you so much for talking to me that night."

Then he left, leaving me with a thousand questions. Another week or two went by, and as I walked through the Arts Center parking lot, I saw him again.

"Hey, man!" I called out as I approached him in the parking lot. "What was that all about the other day in the library?"

"Dude, that story you told me kept playing over and over again in my head. I couldn't stop thinking about it. I was laying in my bed afterward, and I felt what you were talking about in your story! It was so overwhelming, I started to cry! I knew God was real!"

Tom told me how he had grown up Roman Catholic, though in his own words he was "basically an atheist." But when he encountered the presence of God after hearing my testimony, it all changed.

"I've gone to mass every Sunday since you talked to me, man!" he said with genuine excitement.

I got to meet with Tom weekly for discipleship. I gave him his first Bible. And it all began with me awkwardly sharing my testimony with him outside of the Arts Center one night.

Your testimony is powerful. If you have encountered God's love, you need to talk about it. Share your experience with other people. The Holy Spirit will use it to bring transformation. It is the most powerful evangelistic tool you have. Use it.

Every Story Starts Somewhere

If you are reading this and are under the influence of the lies of satan, maybe you haven't yet had your own encounter with God's love.

Maybe you stopped going to church because you believe you don't belong. Perhaps you are constantly under the weight of guilt and fear. Or maybe you believe God's love and hope are for others but not for you. You may even have gone so far as to reject God because you've doubted His goodness.

You are loved more deeply than you understand, and I pray that you will now have the same encounter with the Spirit of Truth that I had. I pray along with the apostle Paul that you "may have power, together with all the Lord's holy people, to grasp how wide and long and high and deep is the love of Christ, and to know this love that surpasses knowledge—that you may be filled to the measure of all the fullness of God" (Ephesians 3:18–19).

If you want to encounter God's love, forgiveness, and acceptance, I urge you to pray a prayer from your heart that goes something like this:

> *Father, I have sinned against You. My sin is great, but I know that Your mercy is greater. I thank You that Your Son, Jesus the Messiah, died and rose again so that I can be free from my sin, my guilt, and my fear. I can't fix myself, but I put my trust in You. You can do what I cannot. Please forgive me of my sin and wash me clean. I want to live a brand new life. Please fill me with Your Holy Spirit, and help me to experience Your love. I receive You now.*

If that was your first time praying a prayer like that, and if you really meant it, I have good news for you: The Bible says you are now "in Christ." You are a new creation! The old "you" is gone, and you are now a brand-new person.

You have been adopted into God's family.

You belong.

If you already know Christ but have been struggling with fear, discouragement, rejection, and hurt, I urge you to pray that prayer again from your heart. Repent (change the way you think) and believe the truth of who God is, what He has done, and who you are because of Him. Your Father loves you, and there is nothing you can do to stop Him.

> For I am convinced that neither death nor life, neither angels nor demons, neither the present nor the future, nor any powers, neither height nor depth, nor anything else in all creation, will be able to separate us from the love of God that is in Christ Jesus our Lord.
>
> *Romans 8:38–39*

Reflection Questions

Journal your answers to these questions or discuss them with a friend.

1. Have you ever felt God's love? What happened? How did you feel?
2. Have you ever dealt with condemnation and guilt? How did you deal with it?
3. Are you still struggling with guilt and condemnation? What are some thoughts and beliefs you hold that have been barriers to your receiving God's love?
4. What is the connection between a personal encounter with God's love and power evangelism?

Action Steps

1. Take some time to meditate on Romans 8:38–39 (see the previous page). Ask the Holy Spirit to reveal the truth of God's love to your heart.
2. Grab a friend and read this chapter together. Practice explaining the love of God to each other. You will find that as you share with your friend, and as your friend shares with you, you will both encounter His love in a powerful way.
3. If you have encountered God's love before (or even if you've just encountered His love today), ask God for an opportunity to share your testimony with someone. Your testimony is the gospel in action. It is one of the most powerful evangelistic tools in your tool belt, so use it often.

CHAPTER 2

Heal the Sick

"I QUIT!" EXASPERATED, I CRIED OUT TO GOD, "IF YOU don't hold up Your end of the bargain, I'm done!"

This was probably the most foolish prayer I have ever prayed, but I was frustrated. You see, since my encounter with God as a fifteen-year-old at camp, I had chased after Him with all my heart. In my zeal, I began to gobble up sermons. I became a podcast junkie, and as I did, I stumbled across a message about evangelism.

A young man began to talk about being bold, taking risks, and taking advantage of every opportunity to share the gospel with a dying world. I was stirred. My spirit began to burn, unified with Christ's, for Him to receive the reward of His suffering: the souls of His lost sheep.

At the time, I worked at a small grocery store in my hometown of Newberry, Michigan. The village of Newberry is a rural community in Michigan's Upper Peninsula. It doesn't have a single stoplight, but for some unknown reason it does have the ability to support the existence of two grocery stores. In their competition for customers, each store did their best to out-do one another in customer service. Each grocery store would not only bag your groceries but would take them out to your car and load them for you. This was my job, and this was what I saw as my opportunity. I began to talk to all of my coworkers about God, and I didn't stop there. If I was your bag boy, you were going to hear me talking about the Lord.

I was obnoxious. I had zeal but no wisdom, no tact, and a very vague sense of self-awareness. I began to argue with people about God's existence. I thought, *Of course, no one can believe the gospel if they don't even believe in God. I had better convince them of God's existence first.*

And so, my pestering began. Would you believe, for all of my boldness and courage, no one was getting saved? I put forth the best arguments I had and got nothing. No one was convinced. It was rather frustrating, but as I continued to listen to sermon podcasts, I came across a preacher who began to talk about healing evangelism. He would pray for the sick, they would be healed, and then there was no need to convince them of God's existence. They had encountered Him for themselves.

What a novel idea! I thought it was such an innovative approach, but as I studied the Scripture I found it was ancient. The precedent had already been set for healing evangelism. In fact, not only was it common in the first-century church, but it was the only evangelism strategy Jesus taught to His disciples.

In Matthew 10:7–8, Jesus is talking to His disciples and essentially tells them, "Look, you have seen what I have been doing for a while now. You have heard the message I preach. Now it's your turn. Go preach the message of the Kingdom of God, heal the sick, raise the dead, cleanse those who have leprosy, and cast out demons." It was the only Jesus-endorsed evangelism method. Nowhere did He tell His disciples to argue. Nowhere was there a command to pass out tracts. I tried but could not find the part of the Bible that tells you to attempt to convince someone that they are super sinful before you tell them about God's love. The only instruction Jesus gave on evangelism was to share the gospel of the Kingdom, and to demonstrate it by healing the sick.

Was I living under a rock? How had I missed this? I had tried every method except what was prescribed by Scripture! I had tried to argue people into the Kingdom of God. I had tried to convince them of their sin and their need for a Savior. But all I got were curt nods, glares, or in the best case, an argument that left me further separated in relationship with the victim of my evangelism than when I had first begun. Why hadn't I tried this? Why had I not even thought of this?

Growing up, I guess I thought that healing was something special that God did whenever He chose. Though I was not a Calvinist, I had a Calvinistic understanding of healing. Every prayer for healing I had heard seemed to be prefaced with, "God, if it's Your will . . . ." I thought that if it was really God's will to heal, it would happen. It wasn't something that could be counted on as an evangelism approach. But as I began to hear testimonies of people being healed, and then coming to Christ, and the more I read the Gospels and the Book of Acts, I began to grow hungry for the power of God to be demonstrated in my life—not because I wanted cool stories, but because people I saw every day were going to hell. I believed this was the best way I could get between them and an eternity without God. And so, I began to pray.

At my job at this little grocery store, I began to pray for the sick. I started off timidly, but before long no one who came into the store on my shift was safe. If you had a limp, a cane, a neck brace, or complained about a headache, I would attack. And do you know what happened? Nothing. Absolutely nothing. Well, I can't say absolutely nothing. In my time praying for folks, I did have two moments where after praying for someone I would see them in church the next Sunday. But the point is, no one was getting healed. I wasn't experiencing what I saw promised to me in Scripture, so I was upset.

I had prayed for countless people over a period of several months, and nothing was happening. I was growing increasingly frustrated with God. I saw in the Bible that if I believed, the sick would be healed when I prayed for them. James 5 told me this, Mark 16 told me this, Matthew 10, Luke 10, and Mark 6 all told me that if I would pray, the sick would be healed—but I couldn't get anyone healed of a stubbed toe.

That's where my conversation with God started. In frustration, I told Him that if He didn't start healing people I would quit. I couldn't keep doing this with no results. I couldn't keep making a fool of myself, putting my reputation, job, and dignity on the line for nothing. I would hear testimonies from people on these podcasts, I would even hear a few from friends, and would grow sick with jealousy and hunger for what they had. "What is it about them, God? I know you don't play favorites, but I am not seeing what they are seeing. If people don't start getting healed soon, I quit." I had no idea that very soon things would change.

"Are you the young man that prayed for me?" an elderly woman asked from behind her grocery cart in the dairy aisle.

"Yeah, I suppose I am," I said, sheepishly curious.

"Well, it worked. I don't need my cane anymore!"

I was overjoyed. I couldn't believe it. I remembered praying for this woman. She had had vertigo for three years. She couldn't balance, so she used a cane to help herself stay on her feet, and when I prayed for her she was healed! It was the first miracle I had ever seen happen through my own prayers, and I was absolutely stunned.

"You should tell everyone!" I said, having no idea what I was saying.

"I did! I told everyone in my pottery class about you!"

I was so excited. I couldn't stop praising God for hours afterward. It wasn't until the next day that I realized I had forgotten to tell her about Jesus. Thank God for mercy. However, God had broken through for me. I finally saw what I had been seeking God for.

I remembered that when I prayed for the woman, I had felt something different. I sensed God's presence as I prayed for her. When I felt His presence, I also had a sense that something happened when I prayed. I wasn't sure if it meant she was healed, but what I did know is that God was there when I prayed for her.

As I looked back on that moment, and the results, I began to realize that what I felt was faith. My faith did not come from looking at the woman's problem and concentrating really hard.

Faith came from an awareness of God's presence in the moment. I felt His nearness and knew in my spirit that something happened. We'll talk more about this later.

Ever since I saw my very first miracle, my "batting average" began to increase. As I continued to step out in risk, miracles began to happen. It wasn't long before word got out, and people actually started to come to the grocery store in hopes they would meet me. One man asked if I was "the praying bag boy." When I said that I was, he threw his leg up on my cart and said, "Pray for my knee; it hurts." I prayed for him, and he was instantly healed! Since then, I have seen even greater breakthrough from broken bones being mended, to brain tumors disappearing, to bone cancer being healed. As I have persevered in seeking God for the gifts of healing, I have found God to be faithful to provide with generosity.

As I look back on that period of life, I realize God taught me a few things. One of these is the principle of persistence. In Luke 18:1–8, Jesus tells a parable about a widow and an unjust judge. The judge refused to give her justice in her case, and instead of saying, "OK, I guess that's that," the woman began to pound on the door of the judge's house demanding justice. Because of her persistence, the judge gave her the justice she sought. The purpose of the parable was to teach us something about prayer. Why is persistence important in prayer?

In Daniel 10, the prophet Daniel begins to pray and fast for his nation, Israel, that the prophecies about the end of their exile in Babylon would be fulfilled. An angel appears to him and says that as soon as Daniel began to set his mind to understand, and to humble himself, he was sent in response to his prayer. However, the angel was wrestling with the "prince of Persia" (a demonic spirit) for twenty-one days.

What's the point? Sometimes our prayers are delayed because of spiritual warfare. There is a war going on around you right now. There is an invasion happening. The Kingdom of God is breaking into this world, and the gates of hell are doing everything they can to resist. Every time we seek the Kingdom of God, we will be met with resistance. And very often, I believe, that is why our prayers can be delayed. This is why Jesus taught us to pray persistently.

In James 5, we read about how the persistent prayer of a righteous person is powerful and effective. James gives us the illustration of Elijah, who was a man just like us who prayed seven times that it would rain, and finally, it rained. This illustration was in the context of James teaching on divine healing. Simply put, James is telling us that when praying for healing, don't give up. Pray like Elijah prayed; be persistent.

Once while grocery shopping with some friends, I saw a woman in a wheelchair. I instantly felt prompted by the Holy Spirit to pray for her, but I was super intimidated because we were in public and I had never seen anyone in a wheelchair healed up to this point. So as a cop-out, I turned to my friends and said, "Do you think we should pray for her?"

My friend Noah, who was bolder than I, said, "Yep!" and walked right up to her.

"Ma'am, we're Christians. Can we pray for you?"

The daughter of the woman in the wheelchair, who happened to be pushing her, rolled her eyes and walked away. I was not encouraged.

I asked what was wrong, and she mentioned that she had some sort of virus that attacked the nerve in her left leg leaving it completely paralyzed.

"Can we pray for it?" I asked, a bit more sheepish than my friend.

"Sure, go ahead," she replied.

I put my hand on her knee and began to pray. After a short prayer, I asked if she noticed any difference.

"Well, I felt a little tingling, but that was it. Thank you for praying for me."

"Could you feel anything before we prayed for you?" I asked, a bit hopeful.

"No, it was completely paralyzed," said the woman.

"So, tingling is good then, right?" I began to get excited.

"Yeah, I guess so," she said.

"Can we pray again?" I asked, a bit more animated than before.

"Sure."

We prayed for her three different times. After the second time, she could feel her toes. After the third time, she could move her ankle and leg. Because she hadn't been able to move her leg, her circulation was poor and her leg was purple and swollen. Immediately the swelling began to go down, and the natural color began to return to her leg!

The woman began to cry and said, "I asked God this morning if He would heal me!" It turns out, He heard her and decided to answer through me and my friends.

I learned a few things about healing leading up to this. First, I learned how to pray for the sick. Often when praying for the sick, we are asking God to heal someone. That is our intuitive method of prayer. Obviously, we cannot heal anyone, so we ask God to do it. The problem here is that is not how Jesus or the disciples prayed. When Jesus prayed for Lazarus to be raised from the dead, He called out in a loud voice, "Lazarus, come forth!" When Peter prayed for the lame man at the Temple gate, he said, "In the name of Jesus Christ of Nazareth, rise up and walk!" Then he pulled him to his feet and the man was healed. There is no record in the New Testament of anyone praying for the sick by asking God to heal. Every time, it is a simple command with the authority of Jesus' name backing up the command. That is how I pray for the sick, and it brings results.

I also learned a few beliefs that bring barriers to healing. If you are able to get rid of these false beliefs, you will see breakthrough. Often in healing ministry, we chalk up our failed attempts to timing issues. We think that God will heal so-and-so at a more appropriate time, because today must be a bad day or something. When Jesus touched the blind man twice, I doubt he was fully healed the second time because Jesus missed the timing by a few seconds. When Elijah prayed for rain seven times, it seems never to have entered his mind that it wasn't raining because he had started to pray too early. Rather, he seemed convinced that his prayer was going to change something as he partnered with the will of God.

Now, sometimes timing can be a factor, but never because it is not God's will to heal. The only record we have of Jesus waiting to heal someone in Scripture is when Lazarus was sick.

When Jesus heard about His friend's illness, He stayed where He was for a few days. When He arrived at Lazarus's house, He knew full well what had happened. Lazarus was four days dead. This was not the end. Jesus, aware of His identity as the Resurrection and the Life, knew He was about to glorify God with the greatest miracle that region had ever seen. It seems to me that God pulls the timing card very rarely, and only when He is about to do something even greater.

The danger of having this in the back of your mind as an excuse for not seeing the miracle is that it prevents you from praying with persistent faith for breakthrough. If Elijah had in the back of his mind the thought that it might not yet be God's will to bring the rain, I doubt he would have prayed too fervently. He was convinced that it was God's will, and it was God's will today. Too often, when the Holy Spirit is actually drawing us to pray with persistence, we think He is waiting for something. Indeed, He is waiting. He is waiting for you to persist. He is waiting on you to believe with enough fervency that He is good, that it is His will to heal, and to heal today, that you will persevere in prayer until His will is done on the earth.

This brings me to a second theological hurdle to gifts of healing being manifest in one's life, and it is a big one. Many people today are sick and are convinced that it is God's will for them to be that way. They don't receive God's healing because they believe God either caused or allowed for the sickness to be there.

This is, in my opinion, the most damaging belief to faith for healing. It is little wonder why those who hold this view of God's will to heal see almost no success in healing ministry. This belief completely undermines one's view of God's goodness and will thwart the sort of believing, persistent prayer that leads to breakthrough in a life of miracles. It is all too convenient to lay the blame for a lack of healing at the feet of God's sovereignty and fail to persevere in prayer until there is breakthrough.

Jesus is the perfect revelation of what God is like. He is the exact representation of God's image (Colossians 1:15, Hebrews 1:3). That means that Jesus perfectly represents the will of God.

Remember the story in the Gospels where the sick man came to Jesus and Jesus said, "Nope. Sorry, this one is from God so I can't heal it. Go home, and allow your sickness to make you godlier"? No? Yeah, me neither. If it seems out of character for Jesus, it should seem out of character for God the Father as well.

Now you may have objections to this point of view, and it is beyond the scope of this book to address each of those, but I maintain that as long as you hold a view of divine healing that allows for exceptions based on God's willingness or unwillingness, you will have only limited success. Of course, there is still mystery. I don't see 100 percent success in healing ministry, but it is interesting to me that those who hold the view that it is always God's will to heal see a much higher percentage of breakthrough in this area. I believe that is because they contend for that breakthrough in persistent prayer in private and accompany that persistent faith with bold action in public. They do this because they know the will of God and have one fewer obstacle to faith than those who believe God allows for sickness in some instances, or are perpetually waiting for "God's timing."

I urge you, if you are seeking God for healing, if you are passionate about evangelism, and if you desire to be used of God in the supernatural and are frustrated with a lack of results, don't give up. Don't be discouraged. Get alone with God, fast and pray (Mark 9:29), and keep praying for the sick. Take risks consistently, and pray and fast in private. Press through the barrier. There is always victory on the other side of discouragement, but you must not lean upon a false theology that allows for inferior results in order to comfort yourself.

I pray that you will be filled with boldness, courage, and strength. I pray that you will never give up. I pray that you will ask, and keep asking; seek, and keep seeking; and that you will knock, and never stop knocking until the door is open. God is faithful, and He always rewards enduring faith.

> Let us not become weary in doing good, for at the proper time we will reap a harvest if we do not give up.
> *Galatians 6:9*

Discussion Questions

1. Have you ever seen God heal someone? If so, please share your story.
2. Have you experienced frustration similar to that of the author in this chapter? If so, please share your story.
3. Are you in need of healing? If so, did you receive any insight or encouragement from this chapter for your situation?
4. What insights or encouragement did you get while reading this chapter as it pertains to healing ministry?
5. What challenges to your current understanding of healing did this chapter bring?

Action Steps

1. Is there anyone sick in your small group or church? Ask to pray for them. If they don't get healed, try a few more times. Pray until either they get healed or get sick of you praying for them.
2. Grab a friend and go to the mall, a grocery store, or some public place. Pray together for a divine appointment, then go out and look for the Holy Spirit to highlight someone. Go talk to them and ask if you could pray for them. If they don't get healed, try praying again.

The Adventure of Saying YES – JonMark Baker

CHAPTER 3

The Gospel

WHAT IS THE GOSPEL, REALLY? WHAT DO WE MEAN when we say we should share the gospel? These are questions I assumed I knew the answers to when I first started my evangelistic endeavors. Sharing the gospel, to me, of course, started with the story of creation. After all, how could anyone believe in Jesus if they first didn't believe that God created the heavens and the earth?

This naturally led to arguments about Darwinism with my unsaved friends and coworkers. I would spend hours evangelizing and oddly enough never got around to talking about Jesus. No wonder people weren't coming to Christ in droves! I wasn't talking about the One who could save them from their sinful lives, from their fear, from their shame and guilt. I was talking about the "how" of creation when they needed to hear about the "why."

Once, when attempting to share the gospel with a gentleman at work, I began to talk about the cosmological argument for God's existence. He listened a bit, but then politely said, "I don't care too much about what happened billions of years ago. I care about tomorrow." I was completely tone deaf toward the needs of the people I was trying to reach. I realized I had no idea how to articulate the truth of the gospel.

I think so many Christians never share the gospel because, in reality, they don't know what it is. The word "gospel" means "good news." It is in its essence the truth of Christ's death and resurrection and what that means for us. The gospel is essentially this: Because of Jesus' death and resurrection, your sins are forgiven, you are healed, and you are a brand-new person whose citizenship is in heaven. All you have to do to appropriate this truth is to renounce your old citizenship to the kingdom of darkness, submit to a new King, and put your faith in Him.

Jesus' favorite sermon was "Repent, for the Kingdom of heaven is at hand!" In fact, it was this very sermon He commanded His disciples to preach.

> "As you go, proclaim this message: 'The kingdom of heaven has come near.' Heal the sick, raise the dead, cleanse those who have leprosy, drive out demons. Freely you have received; freely give."
>
> *Matthew 10:7–8*

One of the problems I've had with the modern power evangelism movement is there has been a lot of emphasis on the power and very little on the evangelism. I've seen YouTube videos, read testimonies, and heard stories of incredible acts of courage and moves of the Holy Spirit as people are taking risks in order to pray for the sick in public places. It's absolutely wonderful. I share many of my own stories of this nature in this book. But very frequently after these amazing power encounters, there is no communication of the gospel. That, to me, is a tragedy, particularly because these two things— the gospel of the Kingdom and the healing of the sick—are intended to go hand in hand.

Why do you think healing was so important to the ministry of Jesus? Many would say it's important because He was demonstrating who He was. He is the Messiah and was proving it by His miraculous signs; that is why the sick were healed. I think that is partially true, but if that were the only reason, it would probably be sufficient for Him to have a ministry comprised entirely of turning water into wine or walking on water. Maybe He was demonstrating His

39

compassionate character? Indeed, I believe He was demonstrating His character through His miracles of healing, but why was it connected to His preaching of the Kingdom? To find the answer, we need to look back to the Garden.

When God created Adam and Eve, He gave them dominion over the earth.

Then God said, "Let us make mankind in our image, in our likeness, so that they may rule over the fish in the sea and the birds in the sky, over the livestock and all the wild animals, and over all the creatures that move along the ground."

> So God created mankind in His own image,
> in the image of God He created them;
> male and female He created them.
>
> God blessed them and said to them, "Be fruitful and increase in number; fill the earth and subdue it. Rule over the fish in the sea and the birds in the sky and over every living creature that moves on the ground."
>
> *Genesis 1:26–28*

When satan deceived Adam and Eve into eating of the fruit of the Tree of the Knowledge of Good and Evil, he fooled them into giving him the authority over the earth. This is why Jesus called satan the "god of this world" and the "prince of the powers of the air." When satan tempted Jesus, he offered Him all the kingdoms of the earth. It would not be a very good temptation if Jesus knew those were not satan's to give. Jesus knew the devil had the power to give Him the kingdoms of this earth if he truly wanted to, because satan's kingdom ruled over the earth through the fall. This is the very reason Jesus came.

In Genesis 3, when God cursed satan for his treachery, God promised that the seed of the woman would crush his head. The Hebrew prophets proclaimed with unified voice that one day the Messiah would come and rule on David's throne, that He would overthrow the kingdom of darkness and establish His rule on the earth. Isaiah prophesied:

> For unto us a child is born, unto us a son is given: and the government shall be upon His shoulder: and His name shall be called Wonderful, Counsellor, The mighty God, The everlasting Father, The Prince of Peace.
>
> Of the increase of His government and peace there shall be no end, upon the throne of David, and upon his kingdom, to order it, and to establish it with judgment and with justice from henceforth even for ever. The zeal of the LORD of hosts will perform this.
>
> *Isaiah 9:6–7 (KJV)*

41

And,

> The Spirit of the Sovereign LORD is on
>   Me,
> because the LORD has anointed Me
>   to proclaim good news to the poor.
> He has sent Me to bind up the
>   brokenhearted,
> to proclaim freedom for the captives
>   and release from darkness for the
>   prisoners,
> to proclaim the year of the LORD's favor
>   and the day of vengeance of our
>   God,
> to comfort all who mourn,
>   and provide for those who grieve in
>   Zion—
> to bestow on them a crown of beauty
>   instead of ashes,
> the oil of joy
>   instead of mourning,
> and a garment of praise
>   instead of a spirit of despair.
> They will be called oaks of
>   righteousness,
>   a planting of the LORD
>   for the display of His splendor
> *Isaiah 61:1–3*

In C. S. Lewis's children's masterpiece "The Lion, the Witch, and the Wardrobe," the white witch had ruled Narnia for years on end. For years it had been winter—always winter, but never Christmas. When Aslan appeared on the scene, the snow began to melt, trees began to bud, and Father Christmas finally arrived. When the witch saw that the snow and ice were melting, the birds were singing, and that spring was beginning to blossom, she began to panic. She was losing her grip on power because HE was here! Aslan was on the move!

This is exactly how the demonic realm reacted when Jesus began to heal the sick, raise the dead, cleanse those with leprosy, cast out demons, and preach those terrible words: "The Kingdom of heaven is at hand." Satan's reign of death was coming to an end, and Christ was demonstrating it when He healed the sick. Every time a demon was cast out, Jesus was demonstrating that He had authority over the god of this world and that the Kingdom of God was going to come and destroy the kingdom of darkness. The Kingdom of God is at hand! Those seven words struck terror into satan's very heart, and they still do.

When Jesus died on the cross, He put to death that which separated us from God. In His death, Christ crucified sin itself:

> God made Him who had no sin to be sin for us, so that in Him we might become the righteousness of God.
> *2 Corinthians 5:21*

Now through His work on the cross, Christ reconciled the world to Himself. Without this work of reconciliation, we would still be bound to sin and under the power of the devil, but

43

Christ put an end to sin's authority over us and offered us the ability to become citizens of His Kingdom.

This is the gospel of the Kingdom. The authority of Christ, His Kingdom, is at hand, and you can enter it! You need only reject your citizenship in the kingdom of darkness and submit to a new King. We who have submitted to the King of this new Kingdom, Jesus Himself, have His Kingdom, His authority, residing within us. Righteousness, peace, and joy in the Holy Spirit have been won for us, because our Redeemer-King paid the punishment for our sin, to ransom us from the kingdom of darkness and the tyranny of death.

George Ladd, in his powerful work *The Gospel of the Kingdom,* expounds the view of eschatological dualism—that is, the "now and not yet" theology. This means that in the gospel, through what Jesus has won for us, we are partaking of the blessings of a future age. Christ is returning one day, and He will once and for all pronounce judgment on satan, sin, and death itself.

Isaac Watts's powerful Christmas carol, "Joy to the World," is an excellent meditation on the rule of Christ when He returns:

> *No more let sins and sorrows grow,*
> *Nor thorns infest the ground;*
> *He comes to make His blessings flow*
> *Far as the curse is found . . .*

He rules the world with truth and grace,
And makes the nations prove
The glories of His righteousness,
And wonders of His love . . .

In the age of the Church, the blessings of this future day are available for those who receive the Good News, that Christ is risen and who become citizens of His Kingdom.

This is the Good News. This is the gospel. Now as we partake of this truth, we are commissioned to be ambassadors of Christ and heralds of His rule. As the apostle Paul puts it:

> Therefore, if anyone is in Christ, the new creation has come: The old has gone, the new is here! All this is from God, who reconciled us to Himself through Christ and gave us the ministry of reconciliation: that God was reconciling the world to Himself in Christ, not counting people's sins against them. And He has committed to us the message of reconciliation. We are therefore Christ's ambassadors, as though God were making His appeal through us. We implore you on Christ's behalf: Be reconciled to God.
> *2 Corinthians 5:17–20*

We carry within us God's Kingdom. His righteousness, peace, and joy reside within the heart of the Christian, and we have the opportunity to draw upon the resources of this

Kingdom to meet all of life's needs both for ourselves and for those around us.

What does this mean, then, for those bound under sickness, sin, depression, anxiety, fear, and shame? How do we communicate the Good News to these people suffering under the power of the devil? We tell them that Jesus has already overcome all of these things. That the suffering they are now experiencing, the loneliness and isolation they feel, the knowledge that there is something more, is actually their heart crying out to experience the purpose of its existence: knowing God! But our sin has separated us from the One who truly gives our lives meaning. But the Kingdom of heaven is at hand. Because Jesus has overcome these things, if we put our trust in Him, submit to His lordship, and invite Him to fill every part of our lives, our sins are forgiven, and we can experience healing and peace. In the Kingdom of God we experience His righteousness, His peace, and the joy of the Holy Spirit. This is the gospel.

I once walked past a restaurant in the town where I live. It was evening, and the restaurant was closing for the day. As I walked past, however, I saw a couple women who were finishing their meal, and I sensed the Holy Spirit leading me to go in and pray for them.

When I reached the table inside, one of the women was in the restroom, and I asked the other if I could pray for her.

"I could really use it," she said, beginning to tear up.

"Do you have a problem in your lower back on the right side?" I asked, believing I was getting a word of knowledge.

"Yes, I do," she replied, a bit confused.

"Do you also have really bad headaches on the back right side of your head?" I asked, feeling slightly more confident.

"Yes. How do you know that?!"

"You have also been feeling hopeless for the last several years due to your finances, and you just had a relationship crash and burn really badly," I said, sensing the presence of God and feeling faith rising up in my heart.

At this point she was weeping with mascara running down her cheeks. She said that was all true, and I began to pray for her.

She was totally healed, and then her friend returned from the restroom. This woman could not have looked more like a fortuneteller from a cartoon if she had a crystal ball in front of her. She had a bandana on her head, no teeth, and various pendants and crystals—which, I assumed, had religious significance—hanging around her neck.

I turned to her and asked if I could pray for her, and she said yes. The Lord revealed to me she had problems in the middle of her back that affected her digestion, and floaters in her right eye.

After prayer, she was completely healed. I then asked if either of them had ever heard the gospel.

"I have never heard that before," said the first woman with a look of confusion and curiosity in her eyes.

I explained that Jesus paid the price for their forgiveness. I shared that we have all fallen and sinned against a holy God, but Jesus has taken the punishment we deserve. He paid the price for our peace, and if we put our trust in Him, and ask Him to be the Lord of our life, we can have true peace.

"Do you want Jesus?" I asked.

"Yes, yes! I need Jesus!" she cried, mascara still running down her face.

That day, I was able to lead her in a prayer to receive the Kingdom of God into her life. I never got to see her again but was grateful I listened to the Holy Spirit in that moment to bring the Kingdom of our resurrected Jesus into this woman's world.

The Kingdom of heaven is at hand for you too. To the extent you submit to Jesus as King, you will receive the blessings of being in His Kingdom. Peace, healing, joy, righteousness, the glory of a new creation, the power of the age to come, and the presence of the blessed Holy Spirit are all available to those who will put their trust in the King of heaven, Jesus Himself.

If you have already received this Kingdom in your life, you are now an ambassador of this

Kingdom. Go and be a witness to the blessings you have received and bring the Kingdom of God to those around you who need it.

Discussion Questions

1. What has been your understanding of the gospel, and how does it differ from the presentation of the gospel in this chapter?
2. Was there any new insight you got from reading this chapter?
3. What is the Kingdom of God, and how does our understanding of the Kingdom of God affect our understanding and preaching of the gospel?
4. What roles do healing and signs and wonders play in the preaching of the gospel?
5. What roles do repentance and faith play in our receiving of the gospel?

Action Steps

1. Try to role-play sharing the gospel with a friend.
2. Read 2 Corinthians 5:17–21 and meditate on what God's will is for you as an ambassador of Christ. Pray about what God would want you to practically change in your life in order to make this truth a reality.
    a. How can you walk this out at work?
    b. How can you walk this out in your family?
    c. How can you walk this out with your friends?

3. Go to a public place where people gather and look for individuals to pray for. Look for the Holy Spirit to highlight people to you. Ask to pray for them and try to share the gospel with them.

CHAPTER 4

What about Faith?

I WAS SO DISCOURAGED! I SAT IN MY CAR IN THE parking lot of the Salvation Army store while my wife was shopping, and I was having a crisis: I sincerely wondered if God would ever use me again. I looked at a woman utilizing a walker, and I knew without doubt that if I were to pray for her, nothing would change. What happened to my faith? Where was my zeal and passion for healing?

This is how it happens, I thought. *This is how someone goes from being anointed of God for healing to becoming completely obsolete. My ministry is effectively over.*

Have you ever been in this place? When you are in ministry, doing things only the Holy Spirit in you can accomplish, sometimes there can be a fear that it's going to stop. This can be especially true after a major disappointment, sin in one's life, emotional burnout, or a demonic attack. I have found myself in this exact place on numerous occasions. While I cannot recall what exactly brought me to the "slough of despair" in this particular moment, I vividly remember crying out to God: "Father, I have no faith! Please help! Don't take Your Spirit from me!"

That's when it happened. A woman limped past my car as I was praying in the parking lot, and I felt the Holy Spirit begin to stir within me. I had a sense that He was highlighting her to me, and faith began to swell. I could almost feel it creeping in like light into a dark room from a door that was just beginning to crack open. My hope that God was not through with me rose as I stepped out of my car and started to search for the woman to whom God had led me.

I looked for the woman and finally caught up to her as she was leaving the store. I asked about her limp, and she said she had been in a car accident. She had extensive surgery in her back with all kinds of pins and screws and rods holding her lower spine together. She was in constant pain, and her medication made it so that instead of excruciating pain, she could hobble with "merely" extreme discomfort.

I asked if I could pray for her, and she consented. While she was not a believer, I suppose that desperation made her willing, even eager to try anything that offered the slightest hope.

I had a sense that the accident and surgeries as well as her limp left her spine misaligned to the degree that one of her legs was quite a bit shorter than the other. I was right, and we found a chair behind the building and I sat her down.

As I prayed for this woman, her leg began to stretch out until it was the exact length of the other leg. I then began to hear the voice of the Holy Spirit. He spoke such specific details about this woman's life. He told me about her other physical issues, that she had shooting pain and carpal tunnel syndrome in her right arm, that she had pain in the upper part of her stomach, that she had ringing and hearing loss in her left ear, and that she had frequent migraine headaches.

The Holy Spirit also began to speak about this woman's life: that she had her heart broken after a divorce or ending of a serious relationship, that they had been together for seven years, and that he had begun to cheat on her and they split up five years ago. The always-compassionate Holy Spirit also began to tell me how this affected her self-esteem. She saw herself as worthless, but Jesus saw her differently. I began to prophesy to her what her value was. She began to weep as the love of God overwhelmed her, but it didn't stop there. The Holy Spirit even told me about her daughters and their destiny and calling from God. I felt like I even got the name of her youngest daughter. I asked if her name was Chloe. "No, it's Zoey," she said. "I was going to name her Chloe, but that is her cousin's name."

I shared the gospel and told her about a great church in the area she needed to get involved in, and we parted ways, both of us amazed at what had just happened.

When I returned to my car, I was in shock. I began to worship and praise the Lord for what He had done. I began to thank Him for His kindness in inspiring faith in my heart and using me in His ministry of reconciliation to a broken and hurting woman. All day long, I was awestruck with God's kindness and overjoyed that the Holy Spirit chose to use me again.

I learned something about faith in that moment. I began to understand more fully what the Scripture says about faith coming by hearing, and hearing by the *rhema* word of God (Romans 10:17). Remember that the word *rhema* has the connotation of an active, living voice. This revelation began to break some misconceptions I had about faith.

Many of us view faith simply as very strong belief. We view it as the opposite of unbelief. And while faith truly is in opposition to unbelief, the two are not diametrically opposite to one another. If faith were the opposite of unbelief, I could work up faith by believing incredibly hard. I have observed that many in the body of Christ hold to this misconception. When they pray for something especially serious, they squint their eyes shut, pray overly loud and overly long prayers, and do their best to work something up. I have found myself in this exact place multiple times. I don't recall a single time I prayed this way where I saw a result. There may have been a few, but I noticed there is a big difference between those moments and the moments when I truly have faith for something.

Faith is the evidence of something not yet seen. It looks like active, quiet trust. While there is certainly a time and a place for loud prayers (even Jesus shouted from time to time), it isn't the volume or length of a prayer that gives it authority; it is the assurance that comes from a word spoken from the Holy Spirit directly to my spirit. Faith comes from God. It cannot be manufactured, it cannot be faked, and it always sees results. The Book of Hebrews, in the King James Version, describes faith as the "substance" of things hoped for. The Holman Christian Bible calls it the "reality" of things hoped for. This is more than strong belief. It is assurance of a reality that is yet to be manifested. But that is not all the Bible has to say on the matter.

The Book of James also tells us that faith always requires action (James 2:14–26). Faith without action is merely an idle notion. Even if you believe that notion with fervent intensity, it is only a thought until it is acted upon and brought into reality. This brings our definition of faith to "an assurance of an unseen reality that can only come from an actively spoken word from God and that brings about fruitful action."

You may now be reading my wordy definition of faith and thinking to yourself, *How in the world does one go about acquiring faith?* If you are like me, you often find yourself in situations where you are anxiously aware of the fact that you simply have no faith for a specific outcome. In those moments, there is a temptation to begin striving in the flesh in order to work up faith. Your prayers get more elaborate and begin to grow in length. You begin to get louder and project authority in your voice—because you know you have none in your heart and you hope this will make up for it. (Come on, you know I'm telling the truth.) And you begin to cry out to God in the situation.

I believe there are at least two different types of faith that a believer walks in. One is gifted, and one is grown. The gift of faith comes from the Holy Spirit and is usually in response to a prompting or word. These are absolutely wonderful, but they are invitations to the second type of faith, which is grown. This type of faith transcends a situational miracle. It is more accurately described as "faith in God" rather than "faith for a miracle." Let me explain the gift of faith first.

Have you ever had a moment where you had faith that you know wasn't yours? I've had times where the Lord strengthened me and I had faith that was not my own come out of nowhere for someone's healing, or a prophetic word, or some other act of service.

I remember being in a park and prophesying over a group of teenagers. I had such faith come on me that I didn't have to ask if I was right. I knew everything I was saying was accurate because it was coming out of my mouth. One of the teenagers was healed, and four prayed a prayer of salvation with me right there on the spot. It was incredible. But that was a momentary gift for a specific purpose. A gift of faith is God giving you His faith for a particular breakthrough. I describe it as the "faith for" kind of faith. I have noticed that after I have had a gift of faith come on me, it increases my expectation to see that particular breakthrough again. God steps in and shows me what He is willing and able to do through me if I would just believe.

The second type of faith I describe as the "faith in" kind. This type of faith can only be grown in relationship. My friend Art Thomas defines faith as "active trust." It is grown in the same way trust in any relationship is built, through intimacy. I trust my wife with absolutely everything, even my son. It's a principle of life that those with whom you are the most intimate are those you trust the most. Now this is where the idea of faith separates from principle and becomes relational.

It would be a perversion of marriage and love itself if I were to marry my wife simply because I wanted a baby and someone to take care of that baby. That is not love; that is convenience. This is the danger of viewing intimacy as a means to the end of faith for healing. When you try to draw closer to God for the purpose of operation in the gifts of the Spirit, you are prostituting your relationship with God to have a ministry. You are taking something that is designed to be relational and making it transactional. That is not a relationship; that is a business.

God did not create Adam simply because He needed a gardener. God created Adam for love. Jesus did not die and rise again so He could have evangelists to tell people about what He did. He did it so He could reconcile the world, you included, to Himself. The Holy Spirit was not given simply for you to be used of God. Instead, according to Romans 8, the Holy Spirit is a seal guaranteeing our inheritance in Christ. He affirms our adoption into God's family, and it is by Him that we can call God "Abba, Father." God put His Spirit in us! Is there anything more intimate than that? We reduce this wonderful truth to mere functionality when we emphasize the aspect of service and gifts whenever we talk about the Holy Spirit.

God could step down from heaven at any point and evangelize the whole world. He could use angels. He could heal all the sick everywhere instantly if He chose to do so. Instead He uses us. Clearly God's priority here was not functionality. The purpose of God giving the Spirit, the purpose of anointing you and me for service, is intimacy.

A common objective builds friendship more than anything else. When God anointed us with the same Spirit Christ had, and when He said that He is sending us in the same way the Father had sent Him, He was bringing us into deeper intimacy with Himself through an invitation to participate with Him in His mission. It is the privilege of the children of God to participate in the mission of God.

When your priorities are right in this area, it becomes much easier to have faith in God for every situation. Your faith is grown because you experience more of God's character, as well as His power. Then you can trust Him for breakthrough no matter the circumstance.

This intimacy can only be cultivated in worship. Worship is more than singing, and it is more than acts of service to God. Worship is an inner attitude of surrender, and this attitude finds a home in thankful hearts.

When we begin to develop a habit of thanksgiving to God, we are training our souls to meditate on the works of God. Since God always reveals His character through His acts, we will naturally begin to praise God for His character.

Praise for God's character will always lead us to submit to Him in worship, because when we understand His worth we are drawn to give to Him what He is worth: that is, our very selves. That is what worship means: giving God what He deserves.

Picture this with me. God has given Himself fully to us. He gave us His Son and left no room for self-preservation. Christ gave it all on the Cross. Then, God filled us with His Spirit. What more can be done? How much more intimate can one be? The ball is in our court. God has made His move, and now it is up to you. You have an open invitation to God's throne room. In fact, you have an invitation to become God's throne room! It is in that place of intimacy that miracle-working trust is grown. Will you accept the invitation?

If you are ready to go deeper with God, pray with me:

"Father, thank You for giving me Your Spirit! Thank You for providing me with everything I need to live a holy life. You are faithful, loving, and good. Your love has no end. I choose to trust You and to submit myself to You as a living sacrifice. I want to give You my whole life, because You are worth it. I want to be used by You, but most of all, I want to know You. Show me Your ways so I can know You and find favor with You. In the powerful, holy, and lovely name of Jesus, amen."

Discussion Questions

1. What revelation did you get about faith while reading this chapter?
2. According to this chapter, where does faith come from?
3. How can you grow in faith?
4. What is the difference between "faith for" faith and "faith in" faith?
5. What is the difference between a lack of faith and unbelief?
6. Have you ever felt like you had no faith at all? How did you process that thought in the moment? How would you process it differently after reading this chapter?

Action Steps

1. Spend some time meditating on God's Word. Faith comes through hearing the active Word of God. Often, we don't hear Him when we read the Bible because we don't take time to listen while we read.

   I like to start in the Psalms, particularly Psalm 103 or 23. First read the whole chapter, then take it verse by verse. Read each verse and prayerfully consider what the Holy Spirit might be saying to you through the Scriptures.

2. Thank God and praise Him for who He is as revealed in His Word. Think about times He has shown Himself to be faithful to His Word in your life.

3. Throughout the day, rehearse in your mind the scriptures you have read. Meditate on the Word of God as you go about your day. Continue to praise Him. You will discover that a reality of God's presence will grow in your heart. All of a sudden you will have faith that grows out of the intimacy cultivated through a meditation on God's Word.

CHAPTER 5

Intimacy

"I DON'T KNOW WHAT IT IS ABOUT YOU, JON, BUT when you are around I can feel it," remarked my unsaved coworker in the middle of the grocery aisle. "It's like there is this peace around you, and I can feel it when you walk past."

Those are words I will never forget. I was truly learning what it meant to live in God's presence and have His presence live in me.

I was working at the grocery store in Newberry at the time, and at seventeen I was finally beginning to discover what it meant to know God. I was so hungry for His presence that I would wake up in the morning, go down to the basement of my house, and spend the first part of my day in worship. I would dance, weep, laugh, and pray. I would then continue in that attitude of worship throughout the day.

It was sweet communion. I was beginning to inhabit by faith the reality that God loves me, enjoys my presence, and actually listened when I prayed. I could feel His presence with me all day. My dad used to say that Jesus is as "near as the mention of His name." I was beginning to truly believe that, and faith arose in me that God was there whenever I set my attention on Him. That faith became the doorway to heaven in me, and as evidenced by my coworker, heaven began to manifest around me, even at work.

I made it my goal to "nourish my soul with high notions of God," as Brother Lawrence is recorded as saying in the book *The Practice of the Presence of God*, and I sought to stay in constant communication with God throughout the day. Prayer to me became a lifestyle, and it looked like continually being aware that He was with me, that He loved me, and that I was pleasing to Him. This awareness brought such a rich depth of communion with God that no matter what situation I was in, I was full of the joy of the Lord.

The hours at work that used to drag on and on at my minimum-wage job would fly by as my heart was enraptured with a sense of God's love. Whether I was stacking cans, bagging groceries, doing dishes at home, or worshiping in my bedroom, I was caught up in the sweetest communion.

Now, lest I paint too rosy a picture here, I have to confess that I was not constantly in this place of God's presence, and I still had moments of failure and sin in my life. But even then, the moment I fled to God for forgiveness, it was as if we were right back where we had left off. To this day, I have whole stretches where I get distracted or discouraged and I lose a bit of that sense of nearness to God. However, I have found that no matter how far I have drifted, the Lord is still near. My dad always says that Jesus is "more committed to you than you are to Him," and I have found that to be abundantly true.

As I grew in my walk with Christ, I began to grow impatient with church people. I honestly became so frustrated with people who came to church and then went home as if they had not been in the very presence of the God of all creation. Sometimes I had much sweeter times of intimacy with God in my basement than at church because the people there had such a low awareness of God. They were more aware of the hunger in their stomachs than they were the hunger in their spirits for the presence of God. Yet I could feel the eagerness of God in my spirit that He longed to fellowship with His people corporately.

It wasn't all their fault, and I probably needed a bit of an attitude adjustment. The reality was they just didn't know, or more accurately, didn't have faith for what I did—that there is a communion with God that is more real, tangible, and special than anything in this world. I had been given faith for something beyond just a good church service, and that faith made me ravenously hungry for what was possible.

I think I was beginning to feel what David felt when he was in the desert of Judah. David, the man famous for loving God, records the longing of his heart in Psalm 63:

> You, God, are my God,
>   earnestly I seek You;
> I thirst for You,
>   my whole being longs for You,
> in a dry and parched land
>   where there is no water.
> I have seen You in the sanctuary
>   and beheld Your power and Your
>   glory.
> Because Your love is better than life,
>   my lips will glorify You.
> I will praise You as long as I live,
>   and in Your name I will lift up my
>   hands.
> I will be fully satisfied as with the richest
>   of foods;
>   with singing lips my mouth will praise
>   You.
> On my bed I remember You;
>   I think of You through the watches of
>   the night.
> Because You are my help,
>   I sing in the shadow of Your wings.

I cling to You;
  Your right hand upholds me.
                        Psalm 63:1–8

David wrote this psalm in the middle of an actual desert. He was literally thirsty for water, but he expressed a deeper longing in his heart for God's presence. Instead of sleeping, he lay awake meditating on God. He was nourishing his soul with high notions of God. Notice the emphasis. David was literally in a desert, but he took the time to write and sing about the meditation of his heart. That meditation was not on the longing of his flesh, but on the longing of his soul. David knew that he could enjoy God's presence, and that intimacy was so amazingly sweet, that he wrote "You satisfy me more than the richest feast" while in the middle of a barren desert hiding from a mad king who wished to kill him.

David writes in another psalm that is recorded in 1 Chronicles 16 to continually seek God's face. This is a command we see over and over again in Scripture, but what does it mean to seek God's face?

I believe the expression is aptly illustrated in Exodus 33. Here we find Moses and God having a conversation after Israel had defiled themselves in honor of the infamous golden calf. God had just delivered the people of Israel out of Egypt, split the Red Sea, and caused all of the armies of Egypt to drown, saving Israel from

Egypt's tyranny forever. God appeared before Israel as a pillar of fire and a pillar of cloud, and in spite of it all, Israel worshiped something their own hands had made, attributing to an idol the acts that their Redeemer God and wrought on their behalf. After this betrayal, the Lord told Moses and the people of Israel that He would not personally go with them into the land promised to their father, Abraham, but would instead send an angel to accompany them.

Many of us would probably be pretty thrilled to discover an angel would be accompanying us as we inherit all of the promises of God. We would think, *How wonderful! Not only is God going to fulfill His promise to me of bringing me into the Promised Land, but He is going to send an angel along with me to assure that I will accomplish the task! Praise God!*

Moses, however, found this to be troubling news. He cried out to God, "Lord, if Your presence does not go with us, do not send us up from here. How else will anyone know that we are your people unless you personally go with us?" Moses was saying that God's presence was more important than accomplishing any goal, no matter how important. Think about this. He was in the wilderness—in the barren, dry, nothing-to-eat, nothing-to-drink desert! He was saying, "God, I would rather die in the desert than enter the Promised Land without Your presence."

Now the word that is translated as "presence" here in the Hebrew literally means "face." It is the same word King David used in 1 Chronicles 16 when he wrote that we must seek God's face continually. This means that seeking God's face, at least to Moses, meant that he put communion with God above every other aspect of life.

Knowing God is what life is all about. Knowing Him is more important than your career. Communion with the Holy Spirit is superior to every other life goal, every other relationship, and every other joy there is, and when you have tasted and seen that the Lord truly is good, you will discover that no earthly pleasure can compare. No wonder the apostle Paul can write from prison to the Philippians that they ought to "rejoice in the Lord always" (Philippians 4:4).

In Acts 16 we read about Paul and Silas in prison. They were thrown in jail for daring to deliver a slave girl from a demonic spirit. The nerve! Suddenly the psychic's owners were no longer able to make money, and they had Paul and Silas arrested and jailed.

I imagine this was not a nice, modern, Western prison either. This was the Mediterranean in the first century. It was probably hot, and sticky, and rat infested. They were jailed and put in shackles. I doubt they were comfortable, and I doubt they were too thrilled with their situation.

Whenever we obey Jesus and it leaves us worse off than we were before, we immediately abandon the idea that it was God leading us. "Isn't God's will for my good?" Yes, God's plan is for our good, but we will be unable to perceive the goodness of God's plan if we are continually defining goodness as comfort. As I read Scripture, it seems to me that God is relatively unconcerned with making us comfortable; in fact, it seems He sometimes goes out of His way to make us uncomfortable. Yes, sometimes obeying Jesus just might land you in prison. This is where we find Paul and Silas.

It's midnight, it's hot, it's sticky, and, in my imagination, there are rats everywhere in the prison. Suddenly we hear two joyful voices quietly singing a hymn of praise to God. Heaven responds with an earthquake. The shackles fall off of every prisoner, and the cell doors fling wide. The jailer, confident that every prisoner has fled, is about to kill himself. But because Paul and Silas are able to discern God's will, they see this as an opportunity for the gospel rather than an opportunity to be comfortable. They share the Good News of the resurrection of Jesus with this Roman jailer, and he and his entire house come to faith.

I want to propose that Paul and Silas were able to rejoice in that prison because they received their joy from God's presence. They sought His face. They sang a hymn of praise not because they were expecting the earthquake, but because they were truly rejoicing in the Lord. Paul and Silas were able to discern the will of God in the earthquake because their joy was not in their comfort, but in God's presence.

Jesus said, "Let anyone who is thirsty come to me and drink. Whoever believes in me, as Scripture has said, rivers of living water will flow from within them" (John 7:37–38). Jesus was talking about the Holy Spirit. When we delight ourselves in the Lord, when we seek His face and drink from His Spirit, we begin to manifest the realities of heaven around us. The internal reality of God's presence in our heart becomes a gateway through which the blessings of a heavenly reality flow to the world around us.

If Christ lives in us, this means we are the place to which people can come to have an encounter with God. To the extent we host the reality of heaven in our hearts, we become a tent of meeting. We as individuals and as a church become the access point through which heaven invades earth.

The reason sick people are healed, the depressed and oppressed are encouraged through a prophetic word, demons are cast out, and the captives of satan are set free on an average trip to the grocery store is not because I am awesome. These things happen because of an awareness of the reality that God is with me. Out of the place of abiding in Him, the fruit of my union with Him manifests (John 15).

My buddy Ken called me one day. In his thick Upper Peninsula accent, he said, "Jon, will you come pray for my wife? She is in the hospital, and we don't know what is wrong with her."

Ken was a biker who came to Christ later in life. He was president of a biker association in the area and came from a rough background. He once told me, "Anything wrong you can think of, I probably did it. I even came close to killing a man in a bar fight once."

When I first met Ken while fishing at the river in Sault Ste. Marie, Michigan, God told me about his knee, ankle, back, and even issues his wife was having. God had healed him, and so he got my number. Anytime he needed prayer, he would call. He was once healed of arthritis over the phone when I prayed for him.

When I got his call about his wife, Rose, I immediately felt the Holy Spirit come upon me. I prayed in tongues the entire drive to the hospital. When I arrived, I saw Ken, Rose, and a third man in the hospital room. This third man was a biker, and he looked rather intimidating. He had a long, braided goatee, a leather vest with several obscene patches, and leather biker boots. Ken knew this man, Mark, from his biker days. Ken had just been telling Mark about the miracles he had witnessed since seeing me, and I knew God had set this man up.

I walked in the room and Mark was looking at me funny, but I decided to ignore it. I introduced myself and prayed for Rose. I then had a word of knowledge that Mark had a problem in his knee, his back, and his shoulder. He asked how I knew that, and Ken exclaimed, "See, I told ya!"

I asked if I could pray for him, and as I did I had several more words of knowledge. God told me that Mark had almost died four times and that God had saved his life every time. He looked at me with wide eyes, and Ken told me about the time Mark had been beaten outside a bar and left for dead.

I asked if Mark wanted to know Jesus, and I was able to lead him to Christ right there. One thing Mark told me, however, has always stuck out to me. He said, "Man, I don't know what it is about you, but when you walked in I felt something. It's like the air changed when you came in this room."

The inner reality of God's presence overflowed into that hospital room because I am a doorway of heaven. When I entered that place, Mark began to feel the presence of the One who walked with me.

If you wish to have communion with the Lord like I have described here, I want you to put your hand over your heart and pray this prayer with me:

> "Father, I know You love me. I know You are with me. I pray that You would fill me with the Holy Spirit. Help me to be aware of Your presence in my life. Give me grace to seek Your face above

*my own comfort. Help me to know that
You truly love me. I want to drink from
Your Spirit, and I want Your living
water to flow from me to the world
around me. In Jesus' name, let it be."*

Discussion Questions

1. What is intimacy with God?
2. What did this chapter stir in your heart?
3. How can you practice intimacy with God in your life?
4. How does intimacy with God affect the world around us?

Action Steps

1. Determine to live a life of intimacy with God. Set practical and achievable goals for yourself. Start with one hour. Try to set your mind on the things of God for one hour straight during your day, then try to expand that time a little longer. Try to see how long you can go without getting distracted. In order to make this work, you will have to feed your soul with something to meditate on, so step two will come in handy.
2. Feed your soul. Meditate on God's Word for an hour. Romans 8 is a good one. Memorize a few verses that stand out to you and spend an hour in your day thinking about them. Listening to a sermon or even some of the stories in this chapter are good candidates

too. Ask God what He might be saying to you through these things.

3. Be thankful. Giving thanks for what God has done, and praising God for who He has revealed Himself to be, is a spiritual discipline that is a gateway to intimacy with God in your life. You will have a really hard time cultivating a life of intimacy with God with a crabby attitude. Thanksgiving and praise lift us up out of a bad attitude and bring us to a place of joy.

The Adventure of Saying YES – JonMark Baker

CHAPTER 6

Stones into Bread

DURING THE SUMMER BREAK BETWEEN MY JUNIOR AND senior years of college, I couldn't find a job. I tried for weeks and decided that if I couldn't find employment, I would work for Jesus. Instead of working every day, I would go out on the streets and look for people with whom to pray or share the gospel. I grew so much in the miraculous that summer. I saw more miracles in those three months than I had seen my entire life up to that point. I would fast and pray, then go out onto the streets and watch the power of God at work. I saw tumors disappear, I saw atheists on the street get healed, I saw people get saved. It was an incredible season. There was, however, a crack in my foundation that began to show during this period of increased blessing.

The first crack appeared when I would go maybe a day or two without seeing someone healed or receiving a word of knowledge. I would begin to fret and worry. I would think, *God is taking away His anointing from me!* I would pray and cry out to God. Then I would intentionally step out and pray for the sick, not for the purpose of loving the person, or to glorify God, but to prove to myself that God hadn't rejected me. If it isn't obvious by now, that is a huge issue, and it began to grow.

After this summer, during my senior year, I started a student ministry at my university called Chi Alpha. I was a student, but my pastor had been talking to me for the past year about starting a Chi Alpha chapter at my school. There was an obvious need for a Spirit-filled ministry at Lake Superior State University, and my pastor believed my friend Lance and I were the guys to make it happen.

I resisted for a while, but during my junior year I heard the voice of the Lord very clearly telling me that I was to start Chi Alpha at Lake State and that I was supposed to do campus ministry after I graduated. I honestly felt unqualified. I had absolutely no idea how to start a ministry, or what I needed to do, but Lance and I decided that together we would trust the Lord and see what happened—and God showed Himself to be faithful.

Immediately we saw God in action. The very things I had seen on the streets in Coldwater over the summer started happening at my school. We saw people healed all over campus. Students came to Jesus, were filled with the Holy Spirit, and our ministry grew. It was an incredible time of breakthrough.

One student showed up to our meeting in my apartment with a walking boot because she had broken her ankle. One of our students, Jamie, was filled with boldness and began to pray for her to be healed. After a few times praying for her, that student left without her walking boot. She was completely healed!

The cracks in my foundation began to increase, however. I was incredibly busy. I don't know if you know this, but ministry is exhausting. On top of starting a ministry, I was a student. I was doing my senior research project, analyzing data for my senior project, going to classes, studying for tests, and doing homework. As if that weren't a full enough plate, I was working a few hours a week, commuting twenty miles to school, and trying to maintain a long-distance relationship with my fiancée, Kara.

At the beginning of the year, I was going strong. I was holding prayer meetings every Friday, evangelistic outings every Thursday, church services on campus every Tuesday, as well as transporting students to and from church on Sunday. I was counseling students between classes and late into the night. If someone called in the middle of the night, I would take the call. If I felt led by the Lord to get out of bed in the middle of the night to pray for someone, I did it.

You might look at this lifestyle and call it radical obedience, but it wasn't obedience. It was fear. I was afraid that if I took my foot off the gas pedal for one instant, I would lose it all. God would be done with me. I couldn't give in to the feeling of tiredness. That was the devil! I had to press through for more breakthrough. More miracles, more salvations, greater fruit!

It didn't take long before this led me to a nervous breakdown. I graduated school with a handful of students left in my ministry. I felt as though I collapsed over the finish line instead of finishing strong. The cracks in my foundation were about to break.

I got home after graduation, with a wedding two months away, and my dad asked me to lead a healing service at his church. I couldn't control it anymore. I began to weep.

OK, I'm going to be real here. I can be kind of dumb. I don't always pay attention to my emotions. The warning signs had been going off for a long time now, and I paid them no attention. I kept driving forward toward more miracles, more salvations, more fruit. *If I don't use it,* I thought, *I will lose it.* When the foundation gave way, and my passion for Jesus and zeal for evangelism began to wane, I couldn't figure out what was happening.

"Why am I crying?" I cried out to God and asked for strength. I couldn't hear God's voice. I felt like I needed to live up to my reputation. I thought I had to be the "awesome man of God" I was last summer.

I began to step out—not in faith, but in fear. Every time I thought I had a word of knowledge, it was wrong. I would ask to pray for people and they would tell me no. When I did get to pray for someone, they wouldn't get healed. Doors were shut in my face at every turn.

Now, you are probably thinking, *Come on, JonMark! Take the hint!* Yeah, I wish I had. My faulty foundation had given way, and I was in a full-blown mental breakdown. I couldn't go to the grocery store without coming very close to a panic attack. I was literally scared of stepping outside of my house because I was terrified of what "God would ask me to do."

Every time I went to the grocery store, I saw every limp, every cane, every wheelchair, neck brace, or downcast face, and I was overwhelmed. I practically ran out of the store on several occasions because I couldn't handle it anymore. What happened to the bold evangelist? What happened to the gifts of the Holy Spirit? I thought the well had dried up. I was afraid I would never be used of God again. Part of me wanted never to be used of God again. I was in a very dangerous place spiritually.

Why am I telling you this story? Because it is important. I learned a lesson through this, and many of you need to learn it as well. The Lord revealed the cracks in my foundation, and I was able to begin dealing with them before they ruined my ministry, my marriage, and my life. What were those cracks? I'll tell you exactly what they were.

The first crack was the unhealthy and incorrect belief that my value to God was based upon my performance for Him. Now, I knew that I was saved by grace. I thought that I knew God loved me, but I discovered something about my motivations. I discovered that whenever I tried to step out in faith, it was in order to prove to myself that I was still anointed.

When satan tempted Jesus in the wilderness, he prefaced every temptation with this phrase: "If you really are the Son of God . . . ." I believe when the devil tempted Jesus to turn the stones to bread, it had little to do with getting Jesus to break His fast. I don't think that was the aim of the devil at all. I think it was to get Jesus to act out of insecurity and doubt.

The tactic of satan was to challenge the identity of Jesus and His relationship to God. He wanted Jesus to act out of doubt and unbelief, and therefore sin against the Father. The devil was trying to get Jesus to perform works in order to prove His identity. Jesus' answer to the devil was this: "Man does not live by bread alone, but by every word that proceeds from the mouth of God."

You have to understand something. This temptation happened right after Jesus was baptized, when the voice of the Father boomed from heaven like thunder: "This is my beloved Son, in whom I am well pleased. Listen to Him." The word the Father spoke was an affirmation of Jesus' identity in relationship to the Father, and Jesus drew His sustenance from the word the Father spoke. The devil immediately began to attack the word that had been spoken to Jesus.

The same trap that was set for Jesus was set for me. But unlike the Master, I fell for it. I began to try to turn stones into bread, because I doubted the work of grace Jesus had done for me on the Cross. It was so subtle, but I had lost sight of the grace of God. I lost the plot. I lost the plot because I was busy. I was too busy. I became so busy that I neglected the secret place of God's presence.

Luke 15:16 says, "But Jesus often withdrew to lonely places and prayed." The Lord Himself had a habit of withdrawing from ministry, from people, from distractions and business in order to spend time with the Father.

Was Jesus less busy than you or me? I doubt it very much. Neither you nor I have had thousands of people chase us across a lake or had people break through a roof in order to get to us. Not many of us have had military officials and people from around the world thronging us in order to get us to come to their houses to heal their loved ones. Jesus was busy! But He knew how to say no to ministry when it was necessary so He could say yes to the Father, and He did it habitually. This is one of my favorite parts of that verse. It says He did it often! The "Word Become Flesh" had a habit of retreating in order to pray. He needed alone time with His Father, and if we think we can do it without that, we are in trouble.

John 15:5 says, "I am the vine; you are the branches. If you remain in me and I in you, you will bear much fruit; apart from me you can do nothing." Ministry and abiding are not the same things. If you are trying to bear ministry fruit, but you are not abiding in the vine, you will wither up. I know from experience.

Because I had neglected the secret place of God's presence, I was no longer abiding in Christ. I was not receiving God's word, which is what gives life to my spirit. Because of this, I lost a sense of security in the love of God and felt the need to earn it through ministry.

The second crack in my foundation was that I had forgotten what the voice of the Holy Spirit sounded like. I thought that nagging coercion was God! I thought the pressing, fearful thought that was shouting in my ear—"If you don't do this, the anointing will be gone"—was God. Because I had neglected intimacy with the Father, I had forgotten His character. He does not lead us like that. The Holy Spirit is gentle. He does not manipulate and extort us into obedience; He leads us. If ever you feel a compulsion to be obedient "or else," you are not hearing God. That is the voice of the evil one.

The third crack in my foundation was that I thought I had to earn the gifts of the Holy Spirit through constant use. I thought that if I let some unspecified amount of time go by without operating in the gifts of the Holy Spirit, God would take them away. The apostle Paul has something to say about this, however, in the book of Galatians:

> You foolish Galatians! Who has bewitched you? Before your very eyes Jesus Christ was clearly portrayed as crucified. I would like to learn just one thing from you: Did you receive the Spirit by the works of the law, or by believing what you heard? Are you so foolish? After beginning by means of the Spirit, are you now trying to finish by means of the flesh? Have you experienced so much in vain—if it really was in vain? So again I ask, does God give you His Spirit and work miracles among you by the works of the law, or by your believing what you heard?
> *Galatians 3:1–4*

If the gifts of the Holy Spirit could be earned, they would not be called the gifts of the Spirit but the wages of the Spirit. This does not negate the principle of faithfulness. In fact, Jesus tells us that if we are faithful with little, we will be given much, and this Kingdom principle certainly applies to spiritual gifts. If, however, you find yourself setting the internal timer after every miracle, making sure not too much time has gone by since your last one, you have forgotten that the Holy Spirit, and His works, are gifts, not commission payments.

It took the Lord literally telling me to spend an entire summer not doing any evangelism at all, and simply focusing on spending time with Him, to reset my system. During this season of rest, the Lord showed me a vision. I saw a vineyard, and it was full of workers who were picking grapes. The strange thing about this vineyard was that everyone in it was laughing. Their faces were beaming with joy as they picked grapes in the Master's vineyard. Then I heard the Lord say, "Everyone who labors in My vineyard does it with joy."

I remember the freedom I felt in that moment. God wasn't interested in me being a slave. He wanted me to rejoice! Serving the Lord should be fun. It should be full of joy and rejoicing. If you are being led by fear, insecurity, guilt, or anxiety, you are not being led by the Holy Spirit. Being motivated by fear is like burning the wrong kind of fuel in your engine. You won't go very far, and you could destroy yourself.

Detoxing from this bad habit has been a process. I can't say I'm never motivated by these things even today, but I have learned some tools to break free.

The first tool is to rest. Create space in your life for longer periods of prayer. This prayer is not to be used for crying out for greater anointing for ministry (that is how I had used a majority of my prayer time). Instead, it is for resting in God's presence, listening to His voice, reading His Word, and enjoying His company. That's it! Just enjoy God. That is what life is all about anyway. I thought the greatest thing I could ever do for God was to lead someone to Christ. That is flat wrong. The greatest thing you could ever do for God is to enjoy Him. The Westminster Catechism says, "The chief end of man is to glorify God, and enjoy Him forever."

If you aren't enjoying life, you're doing it wrong. If you aren't enjoying God, you've missed the point of the gospel. When the Lord was born, the angels appeared to the shepherds at night and announced they had "good news of great joy!" Joy is one of the fruits of walking in the Spirit. If you've lost the joy of walking in the power of the Holy Spirit, you aren't walking in the power of the Holy Spirit. Repent, stop trying to turn stones into bread, rest, and enjoy the grace of God!

If you are feeling burned out, pray this prayer with me:

> *"Lord, thank You for Your love, Your mercy, and Your grace. I know that You love me. Forgive me of trying to earn Your gifts and approval through my own human effort. Forgive me of*

neglecting the joy of intimacy with You.
I choose now to rest in You and enjoy
Your fellowship. In Jesus' name.

Discussion Questions

1. Have you ever been burned out? What was the cause? Why were you pushing yourself so hard?
2. What revelations did you get while reading this chapter? Were there any stories or Scriptures that stood out to you?
3. Have you ever engaged in ministry with the wrong motivations? What were they?
4. How can you change your motivations for ministry if they are wrong?
5. How do you think you could safeguard yourself from burnout in the future?

Action Steps

1. Find a quiet place in your house to be alone.
2. Read John 15.
3. Listen to some worship music that speaks to you.
4. Spend at least fifteen to thirty minutes and meditate on the verses that stick out to you.
5. Take a Sabbath one day a week. This is not just a day for recreation (though that is important); it is a day devoted to resting and enjoying the presence of the Lord.

CHAPTER 7

Trampling Snakes

I have given you authority to trample on snakes and scorpions and to overcome all the power of the enemy; nothing will harm you.

Luke 10:19

THIS IS ONE OF THE CRAZIEST GOD MOMENTS OF MY LIFE, and that is saying something. I want to tell you about my friend Mike (not his real name). Mike was a freshman at the college where I do ministry. I met Mike at a pizza party we threw in the middle of campus at the beginning of the year. Mike's life was about to be turned upside down.

Mike grew up in a Lutheran family, went to a Lutheran school, and knew the Bible fairly well. He came to LSSU, and, like most freshmen, he wanted to have a good time at school. He became sexually involved with a young woman who introduced him to some things that led him into sexual bondage. Later on, he began to date a different girl who began to physically abuse him. He would never fight back, because he never wanted to hurt anyone, but he also had an anger issue, so he was boiling over with rage.

The relationship ended bitterly, as you could guess, and then Mike got a knock on his door. It was campus police telling him that he had a restraining order against him.

He thought, *What?! She is the one who beat me!*

He told me he felt like a soda can that had been shaken, and shaken, and shaken, and finally the can exploded. He screamed at the sky, releasing every ounce of his pent-up rage.

Then it happened. "I can help you get back at her," said a voice in his head.

Like fish in a pond, he took the bait. He began to listen to this voice. He treated it like a friend. He let this voice guide him. He felt empowered by the things the voice encouraged him to do. He felt great, but it was all a lie.

Mike was coming to our small-group Bible study. All of this was happening in secret, and I didn't know all that was going on, but I became suspicious one night when Mike disappeared.

Mike's roommate called me, frantic. He was so worried because Mike was gone and wasn't answering his phone. He was missing for more than twenty-four hours before he resurfaced. We knew not everything was OK but had no idea the extent of what was happening until Mike and I went fishing and he confessed what was going on.

"JonMark, weird things have been happening to me lately," Mike said as we drove to our fishing spot early in the morning. It was still dark, and the cold, late-autumn air made us reluctant to leave the warm car right away.

"What's going on?" I asked.

"I have these spells where I have been falling asleep in one place and waking up in another, and I don't know how I got there."

OK, I thought. *This is probably more than sleepwalking.*

Mike continued, "My roommates told me I was acting weird."

"How so?" I asked.

"They told me I was calling myself by another name. They said I was threatening to kill my ex-girlfriend."

This was new to me. I had encountered demon-possessed people on at least two previous occasions. I knew it was real, but I had never had someone so close to me be so dramatically affected.

"Mike, this is a demon," I said, beginning to grow angry at the devil for daring to put a finger on my friend. With boldness I knew came from the Holy Spirit, I added, "I can get rid of this for you."

"Please do!" he said. "I'm miserable."

I began to pray. Nothing dramatic happened. I rebuked the devil and asked for the peace of God to rest upon Mike. His muscles began to tense up, and he was looking anything but peaceful. I decided to check in with him.

"Mike, how are you feeling?"

Mike gave an unsure response. "Umm . . . I don't know."

"Are you getting angry right now?" I asked, already knowing the answer.

"Yes."

"Does that seem like a rational thing? Does it make sense to get angry right now?" I asked, trying to get him to acknowledge the fact that he was actually dealing with a spirit. He wanted me to pray for him, but he wasn't really convinced he was not just dealing with a mental-health issue. If you don't look squarely in the face of a problem, you will not be able to resolve it.

"Not really," he responded. He was beginning to realize what was happening.

I began to lead Mike in a prayer to God for forgiveness and a command for this demonic spirit to leave. As we prayed, suddenly he felt the spirit depart. He became exhausted and fell asleep in the car for about a half-hour. Then he woke up and we went fishing.

Several days went by, and Mike felt great. But about a week or so later, he asked for prayer in our small-group Bible study. The spirit had come back. I was a bit discouraged, but we gathered around Mike and began to pray.

You need to have an understanding of where we were to appreciate the drama of this scene. We were sitting in a room on the second floor of the university's library. People were studying for exams on the other side of the rather thin walls. Ten or so students gathered around Mike and began to pray that the demon will come out of him. All of a sudden, Mike slammed his fists on the table and screamed in a growling voice, "I WON'T LEAVE!"

Well, that was rather scary for the members of my Bible study. We had brand-new Christians there who never even knew that demons were real. They were a bit surprised, to say the least.

Mike stood up and ran out of the room. I told the student leader to finish the Bible study, and I chased after Mike. I grabbed him as we left the library and said, "We're going for a car ride."

I asked, "What happened? I thought we got rid of this thing."

"I guess not," he said.

I fought down the creeping discouragement. "Mike, have you forgiven your ex-girlfriend?"

"No."

"Mike, I think that is the root of this issue."

I led him in a prayer of forgiveness, and he had another moment of release. He felt the anger leave and the peace of God rest upon him. I drove him to his place and got home rather late into the night.

Mike did well for about a month. He was sleeping at night, and his relationships with his friends and roommates improved. Then in the spring, I got a phone call.

It was back. Mike was in the ER because he was losing it. He had started cutting himself, and this "other guy" was taking over his life. It wasn't just when he fell asleep anymore. He would be sitting in class and this thing would take over. He would often lose several days in a row where he would completely black out and this other "personality" would take over. He constantly had voices in his head, he couldn't stop thinking about sex, and it went even deeper, but you get the picture. This was bad.

Our Chi Alpha student leader, Ben, invited Mike over to my apartment. Ben and I had been fasting and praying. We were sick of this. The demon had taken advantage of our friend for too long, and this was the end.

Mike sat down on my couch. I sat next to him and said, "What is going on?"

"I don't know," he said.

"We've prayed twice, and this thing has left twice and come back worse each time. What are you doing to open the door?"

Mike began to confess sin in his life. He began to truly come to grips with the fact that he couldn't handle this on his own. Up to this point, he had been playing games. He wanted to keep it around when it was convenient because the "other guy" got what he wanted. He liked that power, but it was eating away at his life.

"Mike, are you ready to stop playing games and get rid of this thing once and for all?" I asked.

"Yes, I'm finally ready."

Ben and I began to pray for Mike. We started to pray in tongues. All of a sudden, Mike's face completely changed. He began to laugh at Ben and me. This insidious, demonic laugh began to mock us. I remembered in the Scriptures that Jesus never allowed for demons to control the show. He often commanded demons to be quiet, and so that is what I did.

I pointed my finger right in Mike's face and sternly said, "Be quiet." The demon obeyed and began to just grunt and growl. Ben and I continued to pray in the Spirit and command the demon to leave.

After about five minutes, Mike collapsed on my couch like a dead man. He was completely out. Ben and I continued to pray in tongues. After a few minutes had gone by, Mike woke up.

"How are you feeling, Mike?" I asked.

"It's gone!" he said. "The voices are gone! It's quiet! I feel clean!"

"Is it completely gone?" I asked, wanting to be sure.

"Yes!" Mike said. "It's gone!"

Suddenly, Mike began to look at his arms with wide eyes.

"What's happening?" I asked.

"The scars on my arm are disappearing!" he exclaimed.

I was very curious, but slightly skeptical. I thought Mike was just excited, but then I looked. Mike had a white scar running the width of his forearm. He covered it with his hand for a second, then moved his hand. The long, white scar was now light pink and about a half-inch long. Eventually even that disappeared into normal skin. Every single scar disappeared!

Mike never had another episode. He got free! I learned a lot about the demonic in that one encounter. The first thing I learned was the importance of forgiveness. People cannot be set free from the power of satan and at the same time hang on to their bitterness and hurt.

In Matthew 18, Jesus shared the parable of the unmerciful servant. In the parable, there was a king who had a servant who owed him a great sum of money. It was a debt the servant could never repay. The king had mercy on his poor servant and completely forgave his debt.

The forgiven servant, after leaving his encounter with the merciful king, spotted another servant who owed him a small amount of money. The servant who had just been forgiven accosted his debtor and demanded he pay back the money he owed. The poor debtor begged for more time to pay back his debt, but the unmerciful servant refused. He had him thrown into debtors prison until he paid back every penny he owed.

When the king heard what his wicked servant had done to his fellow servant, he was enraged. He called his evil servant before him and said this:

> "You wicked servant," he said, "I canceled all that debt of yours because you begged me to. Shouldn't you have had mercy on your fellow servant just as I had on you?" In anger his master handed him over to the jailers to be tortured, until he should pay back all he owed.
>
> *Matthew 18:32–34*

Jesus finished his story with some chilling words: "This is how my heavenly Father will treat each of you unless you forgive your brother or sister from your heart."

Mike told me that his hatred toward his ex-girlfriend was the gateway through which satan gained access. Jesus said that those who don't forgive are like the unmerciful servant who refused to forgive and was then handed over to the jailers to be tortured, and his debt was reinstated.

Here's the deal. You cannot operate in the economy of grace and the economy of vengeance simultaneously. Everyone wants mercy for their own sins, but no one wants the one who wronged them to get merciful treatment—but you cannot have it both ways. Either you have mercy all around, or no mercy at all.

When Mike was holding hatred in his heart with a refusal to forgive, he was "handed over to the jailers to be tortured." The devil had access because Mike refused to forgive. When Mike finally confessed his sins, and forgave his ex-girlfriend, he was set free.

The demonic can also be behind a lot of physical infirmities. In Luke 13, Jesus saw a woman who was crippled with severe scoliosis. Jesus recognized that she was bound by the power of the devil. He laid hands on her and declared that she was freed from her infirmity.

I have seen unforgiveness open the door to the demonic in people's lives and when they truly forgive, they are immediately healed. One young woman was wheelchair-bound because of a back issue. After prayer, the pain grew worse. I had a sense that she needed to forgive someone in her life. She confessed that her dad had abused her. She confessed her anger and bitterness toward her father, and when she forgave, the pain immediately left and she began to walk completely pain free.

Secondly, I learned that getting free and staying free were completely different matters. Jesus said something rather mysterious about people who are delivered of demons:

> "When an impure spirit comes out of a person, it goes through arid places seeking rest and does not find it. Then it says, 'I will return to the house I left.'

When it arrives, it finds the house
unoccupied, swept clean and put in
order. Then it goes and takes with it
seven other spirits more wicked than
itself, and they go in and live there. And
the final condition of that person is
worse than the first. That is how it will be
with this wicked generation."

Matthew 12:43–45

When Mike got free the first time, I was so
excited. I was very discouraged when the spirit
came back worse, but then I remembered those
words of Jesus. I realized this was what the Lord
was talking about. When Mike got free, he
refused to truly repent of his hatred. He thought
he could handle it, and he sort of enjoyed the
sense of power he got from the demonic spirit.
He was still a rather hospitable host to the
spiritual parasite that was ruining his life.

It wasn't until Mike realized that he actually
could not handle this on his own that he truly
was set free. Mike humbled himself, confessed
his sin, stopped playing games, and truly
repented, and he was completely free. If you are
casting out a demon from someone, have a chat
with them first about hatred and unforgiveness.
It will be impossible for them to truly be free as
long as they are operating in the economy of
vengeance.

Third, I learned some practical things about
casting out demons: Develop a lifestyle of fasting
and prayer, praise the Lord during the entire

deliverance confrontation, and pay minimal attention to demons.

When Jesus came down from the Mount of Transfiguration with Peter, James, and John, He found a rather chaotic scene. The disciples had been trying to cast out a demonic spirit from a little boy, but they couldn't. Then the Pharisees, always eager for an opportunity to try to make Jesus and His followers look bad, started an argument. Meanwhile a demonized and epileptic boy and his distraught mother were standing by just hoping for freedom. Jesus arrived, and cast out the demon.

Later, Jesus' disciples asked why they couldn't cast the demon out of the boy. Jesus gave two different reasons why they couldn't: because they had such little faith, and because they hadn't developed a sufficient lifestyle of prayer and fasting. I would argue that those two reasons are actually related.

In prayer and fasting, we are setting aside our consciousness of the flesh in order to seek the Lord. As we do that regularly, we are training our minds to be conscious of God. This is where faith grows. The more aware we are of God, the more faith we have that He is strong enough to overcome any obstacle. We have no authority over demons apart from faith in Christ's power. Now demons will do everything they can to thwart faith, and that brings me to my next point.

Jesus routinely commanded demons to be quiet. Why? Because they try to steal the show.

By putting on a show they attempt to intimidate, manipulate, discourage, and distract. They try to make themselves seem bigger than God. The devil has been doing it from the beginning, and that is still the number one tactic.

The solution here is simply to keep your eyes upon Jesus. You can proactively do this with worship and praise. Keep your eyes upon the King of Kings who has all authority in heaven and on earth. Stay consciously aware of the presence of the Holy Spirit, then, from the peace of God's presence, command with the authority of Jesus' name that the demon be quiet and come out.

Some demons come out immediately. Jesus cast out demons with one word. That is awesome! He also had a few moments where He commanded a demon to come out, and the person fell down and shrieked for a while before the demonic spirit left (Mark 1:23–26). I've had deliverance sessions take anywhere from five minutes to two hours. If it is taking a long time, don't get discouraged. Talk to the person to confirm there is nothing they are holding onto that is impeding the deliverance, keep your eyes on Jesus, and keep at it. The demon would not be manifesting and throwing a temper tantrum if its seat of authority was not threatened. The fact that the demon is manifesting is a sign that the person is close to freedom.

A few notes of caution here. When the little boy didn't get free, Jesus never blamed the boy.

He encouraged the disciples to have more faith and to pray and fast more. If the person is not getting free, it is so vital that you don't blame them. That can be tempting to do if you are concerned about your reputation as a man or woman of God being tarnished by a failure, but the reality is, Jesus never blamed the victim.

Now it is true that sometimes people truly don't want to get well, and in those cases, total freedom is not likely; and if it does happen, the demons will come back. However, just because someone didn't get free doesn't mean it was their fault. It is easy to blame the other person. It is hard to look in the mirror and say, "Lord, help my unbelief," but that is the place of power.

Discussion Questions

1. Have you ever had an encounter with a demonic spirit? What happened?
2. What do you think are some common gateways to the demonic in people's lives?
3. Have you ever experienced unforgiveness and its negative effects in your life? Were you able to forgive? If not, why not?
4. How often do you think physical sickness can be associated with the demonic?

Action Steps

If you have unforgiveness in your life, it is time to let it go. A good exercise for this is to pray and ask God to reveal any areas where you are holding onto bitterness. I want you to close your eyes and picture the person's face as though they were standing in front of you. Look them in the face and tell them, "I forgive you, and you owe me nothing." Pray for that person and ask God to bless them.

You may still be angry, but forgiveness is an act of the will. Forgiveness is something you choose to do. As you make the choice, the feelings will follow. This will be a healthy step toward freedom.

Ephesians 4:26–27 says, "'In your anger do not sin': Do not let the sun go down while you are still angry, and do not give the devil a foothold." If you allow anger to fester, you are giving place to the devil. It's time to step into God's freedom.

The Adventure of Saying YES – JonMark Baker

CHAPTER 8

'You Should Be a Psychic!'

"MA'AM, DO YOU HAVE PROBLEMS IN YOUR LOWER back, right hip, and right knee?" I asked the woman smoking outside of the psychic shop.

"No," she replied curiously.

Uh oh, I thought. *I really blew it this time!*

You see, I'd driven by this particular psychic shop several times. It was right around the corner from my church in the Metro Detroit area. After my wife, Kara, and I got married, we moved to Taylor, Michigan, and I had been seeing more psychic shops than my sheltered, rural mind could have ever fathomed actually existed.

Almost daily I drove past this particular shop, and my imagination would go crazy. I thought I could stroll in there in the power of the Holy Ghost, call out the demonic powers like Carman in his "Satan, Bite the Dust" music video, have an Elijah-type showdown with these psychics, and God would manifest His power.

Surprisingly I felt like the Holy Spirit was giving me the "red light"—probably because of the pride and selfish ambition that was motivating those thoughts, rather than the love of Christ (2 Corinthians 5:14). However, I believe the Holy Spirit saw that I did want to glorify Jesus, so one day that red light turned green.

I was driving north on Telegraph Road on my way to the church, and I felt a strong unction from the Holy Spirit to go to the psychic shop immediately. I felt it was urgent and to wait would be deliberate disobedience to the will of God.

I dropped Kara off at the church and said, "Hey, babe, God is telling me to do something. I'll be right back." She had absolutely no idea what was going on, but I didn't have time to explain.

As I drove there, I had an impression, or a "gut feeling," that there would be a woman with lower back pain and problems in the right hip and in the right knee, and someone else with macular degeneration in the right eye.

I pulled into the parking lot and saw a couple, each wearing interesting-looking pendants, smoking outside the shop. Bingo! These people were obviously psychics and were definitely the reason God had sent me.

I smiled my best smile and in a jovial manner said, "Hey, guys! This may sound strange, but I am a Christian, and I felt like God wanted me to come and pray for you and tell you how much He loves you!" That is when I boldly asked the woman about her back, hip, and knee.

"No," she said. No? I felt so strongly this was God. I was so bold approaching these psychics. How could I have missed it this badly? Time to abort!

"It's my left leg," she said, still curious.

Close enough! I thought, relieved that I wasn't completely off.

"Could I pray for it?" I asked.

She said yes, and I put my hand on her shoulder and began to pray. As I did, I got a download from the Holy Spirit. I began to tell this woman about her headaches, that when she gets them her ears ring, that she has a problem in her left wrist, even about some dreams she had the previous week—and that they were a message from God.

The man standing next to her, himself a psychic and, I found out later, this woman's husband, stared with eyes wide. "You should be a psychic!" he said, in shock. "You could make so much money doing this!" I explained that I was a missionary and received my revelation from a different spirit than they did.

"I get my revelation from the Holy Spirit," I told them as gently as I could. "He is pure love and isn't about manipulation at all."

The woman was completely pain free after I prayed for her, and I asked the couple if anyone in the shop had macular degeneration in their right eye. The man exclaimed in disbelief, "That's me!"

I prayed for them and shared the gospel with them, though they were surprisingly unreceptive. I told them about my church and its food bank and healing rooms. "If you ever need anything or are in need of physical healing, you are more than welcome to come," I told them.

"Well, we have needy clients that come in all the time. We can just refer them right to your church." That's right—the psychic shop began to refer people to my church!

At the psychic shop, the Holy Spirit was demonstrating the love of Christ through one of the prophetic gifts called the "word of knowledge" (1 Corinthians 12:8). The word of knowledge is an incredibly powerful tool the Holy Spirit gives us. It is used, among other purposes, to encourage the saints, convince unbelievers, and to increase faith, either for healing or to prepare someone's heart for a word of prophecy. Simply put, the operation of the word of knowledge is where the Holy Spirit reveals information that was not obtained through natural means. This type of prophecy is present throughout the Bible.

In Acts 9 we read the story of how Saul of Tarsus is transformed into Paul the apostle. The Lord appeared to Saul and spoke to him. Saul was struck blind and was led to the house of a man named Judas. Then, we read that the Lord called to Ananias in a vision. Ananias was told to go to the house of a man named Judas on Straight Street. He was told to talk to Paul because he had been struck blind, to pray for him, and that he would receive his sight.

What a prophetic word! It was incredibly detailed and was used for the purpose of preaching the gospel and discipling the man who would become the great apostle Paul.

This gift first manifested in my life when I was seventeen. I received prayer at a conference from a man who operated in this gift. When he laid hands on me, the power of God came upon me and I was overwhelmed. I could no longer stand, so I fell to the floor, and when I did the peace of God rested upon me.

Later that evening, I was asked to pray for a friend of a friend. When I did, I felt led to pray for his anxiety and for his relationship with his father. It so happened that he was on medication for anxiety and had significant issues in his relationship with his father, which affected every area of his life. I couldn't believe that God just spoke to me, and through me. I was so excited.

God will speak to us in incredibly diverse ways. Each person is unique, and God seems to speak to people by means that reflect his creativity and personally intimate relationship with each individual. Some people feel pain in their body that is not theirs. It is actually the Holy Spirit letting them know what someone else is experiencing. Some receive impressions, or gut feelings. Others will see pictures either in their minds or with their eyes. For instance, sometimes I will see in my imagination a dark spot over an area of someone's body. That is usually a word of knowledge that someone is dealing with an issue there.

Typically, I receive words of knowledge as an impression. Have you ever prayed for someone and felt like you should address some specific need of which you had no natural knowledge? I also will frequently have a picture in my imagination that will pop up when I am praying or in some way engaging the presence of God.

Once, I was praying for people at my church's food bank, and I felt faith to prophesy. I had a sense God was going to use me, so I went out to the line and God pointed out a woman to me. I can't explain how I knew God was leading me other than the fact that I felt drawn to pray for this woman.

I approached her and asked to pray for her and she said, "Yes, I was just contemplating going to receive prayer."

I began to pray for her without asking what she needed, and the word "autism" appeared in my imagination in block letters. With that came the thought that her son had autism.

I was not 100 percent sure this was God, but I didn't give myself time to reason it away. I asked if she had a son who was sick, and she said yes. I then asked if he had autism, and she began to tear up and said, "Yes, he does." I told her God was with her and encouraged her as I prayed for her son's healing.

Then I saw the word "cervix" in my imagination, and, emboldened by my previous word, I told her, "There is a mass on your cervix, and the doctors don't know what it is, but God says not to worry about it. You will be fine."

She was blown away and with tears in her eyes thanked me for praying for her.

There are numerous ways in which God can talk to us, and we need to pay attention to them. Often we can miss it if we lock in on one particular channel. If I am getting an impression from God but don't step out because I didn't get a picture, I am missing God.

If I were a gambling man, I would wager that you are reading this thinking, *Man, I wish God would speak to me that clearly and specifically! I want words of knowledge like that.* I want to share with you three principles that, when I understood and acted upon them, enabled me to grow in the gift of the word of knowledge.

First, I needed to understand that God wants to give me words of knowledge, and I need to expect them. Romans 12:6 tells us to prophesy in accordance with our faith. That means I need to be aware that God is already speaking to me and that I can tune into His voice by reaching out in faith to hear Him.

After becoming a full-time campus missionary, I have had multiple opportunities to step out intentionally and try to hear God. I remember being in the basement of our student union and running into one of our Chi Alpha students, Charlie, and his friend, Alicia. They were playing pool, and I was wandering around campus and happened to run into them. I started chatting with Alicia and asking what her major was, but inwardly I was stretching out in faith, asking God to speak to me.

She talked about getting migraines frequently, and I saw my opportunity. I asked if I could pray for her, and Charlie gave me the look. He knew what was about to happen. She said yes, and I had an impression that she also dealt with chronic lower-back issues and some stomach problems. God also told me that she had dealt with some demonic issues, which affected the way she viewed herself. I had a short movie play in my head of her driving, and from the passenger seat she heard a voice speak to her that she was worthless.

When I shared that, her eyes grew wide and she confessed that it was true. After prayer, her back pain was healed, and she immediately began coming to our Chi Alpha small-group meetings. It wasn't long before I got to lead her to the Lord and baptize her. She is serving the Lord to this day.

It all began not because I had a voice from God interrupt me, but because I was looking for the opportunity and reaching out in faith, expecting Him to speak.

Second, I learned to discern what God's voice often sounds like. I was once in a conference where someone described God's voice as having an accent. It is true that God's voice has an accent, and His accent sounds like compassion, love, and, most importantly, faith. Romans 10:17 tells us that faith comes by hearing the *rhema* word of God. This means that when the living voice of the Holy Spirit is spoken to our hearts, faith is activated. Every time I hear the voice of God, there is a measure of faith that comes alive in my heart.

How, then, do I know God is speaking to me? I listen for faith. When that tiny spark of faith comes, I know it's God. God's voice also carries with it the attributes of God. You know the Holy Spirit is speaking to you when you are suddenly moved with compassion, or when you sense the peace or presence of God's Spirit.

God's voice is rarely demanding. When He speaks to us, He doesn't harp on our insecurity to manipulate us into obeying. That is the devil. Any time I sense fear that says, "If I don't pray for that person, I am a terrible Christian," I shut it down immediately. If I begin to follow that voice, I will quickly find myself burned out, worn out, and motivated by fear rather than by Christ's love for myself and for those around me.

The third principle I've learned is that I needed to lower the standard of how sure I have to be before I take a risk. John Wimber famously said that "faith is spelled R-I-S-K." Most of us have a threshold of how strongly God has to speak, and how sure we are that it indeed is God, before we are willing to take a risk and step out with what we believe God has given us. Faith grows as you lower that threshold and begin to take risks.

Often when I step out with a word of knowledge, I am maybe sixty percent sure it is God. That is OK. I am willing to be wrong and look like an idiot, because more often than not it *is* God. Taking risks like that requires a little humility. You must let go of any compulsion to save face. If you give yourself permission to miss it sometimes, you will greatly increase your ability to grow in the gifts of the Spirit.

I believe God is more interested in your attempts than He is in your successes. My grandmother once told me, "God is more interested in the minister than He is the ministry." That means He is just as pleased with your failures as He is your successes, because failure is a sign of growth. I still miss it sometimes when it comes to words of knowledge. When I miss it, I don't accuse the person of lying to me (even though sometimes they are), and I don't beat myself up for failing. Instead, I thank God that I was at least willing to try, and I ask Him to help me continue to take those risks. I intentionally try to see my failure from His perspective.

God is our Father. Any father who sees his child fall while trying to walk doesn't berate his child for falling, but rejoices in the fact that the child tried. That is the way God sees us. He wants you to succeed. He is your biggest cheerleader. He loves you more than you will ever know. Since all this is true, how can you lose? "If God is for you, who can be against you?"

I pray that God will empower you by His Spirit to prophesy, that you will be filled with the Holy Ghost and begin to manifest those gifts for the sake of the world around you. I pray that you will humble yourself and give yourself permission to take risks and grow. Go! Make mistakes! Bless them with the grace God gives you, and learn for yourself how to hear God's voice.

Discussion Questions

1. Have you ever heard the voice of God? What did He say? What did it feel like when you heard Him?
2. How does Jesus typically speak to you?
3. Have you ever had a word of knowledge for someone and shared it? What happened?
4. Have you ever thought you had a word of knowledge for someone and were wrong? How did you process it?

Action Steps

1. If you are in a small group, have everyone pray for a minute for the person to their left. Have them ask God for a word for that person, then have them share whatever it was that came to mind. Don't filter; this is a safe place to fail. Share any pictures or thoughts that come to your mind.

2. Try listening to God for your server next time you are in a restaurant. Ask God to give you something for them, and try sharing it with them. Be humble, be willing to be wrong, and don't be weird. This is a great way to practice hearing God's voice and may lead to an amazing God encounter.

CHAPTER 9

Inconvenient Adventures

"I WAS IN THE GROCERY STORE . . . ."
This seems to be how every one of my testimonies starts. I have seen more people healed, saved, or prophesied over in the grocery store than practically anywhere else. I have decided that I would make saying yes to the Holy Spirit part of the rhythm of my day. He has permission to interrupt me at any time. But let me finish telling you the story.

I was in the grocery store. While walking through the cereal aisle, the Holy Spirit highlighted two women to me. I immediately knew one of them had a problem with her shoulder and her back, so I approached them and said, "Excuse me, ladies. This is a strange question, but do either of you have a problem with your shoulder and back?"

Looking a bit confused, one of the women said, "Yes, I do. Why do you ask?"

"I am a Christian," I replied, "and I love to pray for people. Sometimes I get a sense from God that someone is dealing with something and that I am supposed to pray for them, and that is what happened just now. Could I pray for you?"

"Sure," said the woman who had the pain.

"Before I pray," I said, turning to the other woman, "do you have migraine headaches, pain in the upper right part of your stomach, and problems in your right knee?"

A bit stunned, she said, "Yes, I do." Then the dam broke. A sense of faith filled my heart, and I knew I was seeing by the Spirit. I told these two women about practically everything in their lives. I saw that one of them had problems sleeping, relationship issues that were caused by lies of self-doubt, and that she actually heard a disembodied voice lie to her about her self-worth.

Then I turned to the first woman and told her she had problems sleeping for the last three years and incredible anxiety for the last seven months. I prayed for them, and they were both healed of any pain they were experiencing at the moment.

The second woman turned to me and said, "We were just having lunch this afternoon, and I told her that I couldn't believe in God or heaven or hell without any evidence." It would appear God was listening.

This was an incredible God moment, but it is a typical trip to the grocery store for me. I have seen almost this exact scene play out in the grocery store, in the drive-through window, in the movie theater, on the college campus where I minister—even in church! This is what happens when you are willing to say yes to the Holy Spirit on a daily basis.

Once, God told me about the chronic headaches, anxiety, and back problems the woman in the drive-through window was experiencing. She began to cry. I didn't even pray for her but just said, "God is healing you," as I pulled to the next window. Later I went to the same place and saw her again, and it turns out that God had indeed healed her.

Many of the miracles that took place in the New Testament happened while Jesus or one of the apostles was going somewhere else. A blind man was healed on the road out of Jericho. A lame man was healed as Peter and John went to pray at the Temple. If you look at the Book of Acts, it can almost be seen as a series of God interrupting people on their way to somewhere else. The Holy Spirit has so many adventures waiting for us if we are simply willing to be interrupted.

In Acts 8, we read about Philip the evangelist. Philip is in prayer, and an angel appears to him and tells him to go to the road from Jerusalem to Gaza. This is interesting to me, because I have discovered this is exactly how the Holy Spirit directs me. He almost never tells me what I am going to encounter and never lays out the full plan, but gives me directions like a GPS—that is, step by step.

Philip obeys and sees an Ethiopian eunuch on the road. Then the Holy Spirit tells Philip to go and walk near the chariot. When Philip approaches the chariot, he hears the eunuch reading from the Book of Isaiah. What a setup! The Holy Spirit leads Philip into position for an alley-oop!

Philip engages the man in conversation and asks if he understands what he is reading. Exasperated, the eunuch replies, "How can I, when I have no one to explain it to me?"

Philip starts there and begins to expound the gospel of Jesus to him. The eunuch puts his faith in Christ, becomes a Christian, and is even baptized. As soon as the eunuch comes out of the water, Philip disappears and is transported by the Spirit to Azotus. He begins to preach the gospel everywhere until he reaches Caesarea.

Philip was a man who created space in His life for the Lord to interrupt. Imagine if Philip had said, "You know what? I'm kind of tired. I don't want to go all the way out there. Can you at least tell me why you want me to go out there?" He would have missed out on an amazing adventure and would have been disobedient to God.

I remember when I was just beginning to follow the Holy Spirit in the lifestyle of evangelism. I was seventeen and was walking home from the grocery store that was a few blocks from my house. I walked behind the abandoned building, and in the empty parking lot was a kid I had met once. He was an intimidating character and was playing hacky sack by himself.

I immediately had the thought that I should play hacky sack with him and talk to him about Jesus. I was scared and began to reason away what I knew in my heart to be the leading of the Holy Spirit. You know it's the Holy Spirit when you begin to argue vehemently with yourself, and boy, did I. I began to tell myself that the thought was just my imagination in spite of the burning in my heart that was pushing me to go and talk to this guy.

I successfully ignored the Holy Spirit and got to my house. It was a Wednesday, and I had youth group that night. I led worship for my youth group and was excited to do so that evening. I grabbed my guitar and began to practice the songs I was going to lead for youth group, and that is when the Holy Spirit scolded me. I heard the very clear voice of the Holy Spirit speak to my heart, "So, you'll worship Me, but you won't obey me?"

Wow. I was so sobered by that rebuke that I immediately put my guitar down, found the kid, and talked to him about Jesus.

Following the voice of the Holy Spirit is a serious matter. Once in my little town, I was led by the Holy Spirit to talk to a woman about Jesus. I chickened out, and I saw her obituary in the newspaper the next week. When God wants to step into people's lives, He does it through His people. The Holy Spirit does not lead us to do things that don't matter. When He decides to interrupt our lives, it's always for a purpose, and it is always worth the interruption.

In John 21, Jesus has died and risen again. Peter, though, is still disappointed with himself for denying the Lord Jesus before a servant girl. He decides to go fishing, and the rest of Jesus' disciples go with him. They are out all night and don't catch a single fish. As dawn breaks, a voice calls to them from shore asking if they had any luck. Peter replies that they had not. The voice tells them to cast their nets to the other side. When they do, they haul in a catch that is too big for the boats to carry. Then we read something powerful:

> Then the disciple whom Jesus loved said to Peter, "It is the Lord!" As soon as Simon Peter heard him say, "It is the Lord," he wrapped his outer garment around him (for he had taken it off) and jumped into the water.
>
> *John 21:7*

No one recognized that it was Jesus, but "the disciple whom Jesus loved" did! Do you see it? The disciple who laid his head on Jesus' chest, the one who never left his side, the one "whom Jesus loved" recognized the voice, character, and appearance of Jesus before anyone else. Those who are intimate with God can discern Him in any situation. Those who know God will recognize His voice, will be aware of His presence, and will be sensitive to His leading, whatever the circumstance.

Those who are intimate with God create space in their lives for God to interrupt them. When they are at the gas station, they are sensitive to the leading of the Holy Spirit. When they are grocery shopping, they are aware of those around them and attentive to the Lord's direction.

In the church tradition in which I was raised, I was often told that the church service should be led by the Holy Spirit, that the Holy Spirit should direct the singing, the preaching, and the order of service. We valued God's leading in our church services so highly. This is a great thing. I love it when the Holy Spirit is the orchestrator of our church gatherings, but as important as it is to have the Holy Spirit direct our church gatherings, it is just as important to have Him direct our gas pumping, grocery shopping, parenting, our time at work, our everything! If you want to have adventures with

Jesus, invite Him to interrupt the rhythms of your life. Evangelism doesn't always have to be an event. When you are filled with the very Spirit of God, when you carry the authority of His Kingdom with you everywhere you go, you are authorized to do Kingdom work at any given time or place.

The title of this book is *The Adventure of Saying Yes* because that "yes" to the Holy Spirit when He wants to interrupt you or inconvenience you is always the first step of every adventure with God. If you want to be used of God, you must give Him permission to interrupt your routine. Invite Him into your daily rhythms, and approach every day with an expectation for Jesus to interrupt your day with an adventure.

Discussion Questions

1. Have you ever had the Holy Spirit interrupt your day? Share the story. What did it feel like when God was speaking to you?
2. Have you ever had God "highlight" someone to you? What did it feel like?
3. What are some revelations you got while reading this chapter?
4. Have you had moments where God was leading you, but you didn't realize it was Him and ignored it? Why did you doubt it was God speaking?
5. How can you be more sensitive to God's leading throughout the day?

Action Steps

1. When you wake up in the morning, ask God to interrupt your day. Pray for a divine appointment, then look for the person God is highlighting to you throughout the day. It could be anyone. Keep a lookout for the person God has for you. Make this a habit. Try every day to be sensitive to God's leading everywhere.

2. When you go grocery shopping, pray before you go into the store. Ask God to highlight someone to you while you shop. When you feel drawn to someone, pray for courage, then go and approach them. I usually start with something like this:

    "Excuse me, ma'am. This may sound a little strange, but I am a Christian, and I love to pray for people. Sometimes God puts people on my heart when I walk past them, and I felt like He was putting you on my heart. Is there anything I could pray with you about?"

    Then I will share any words of knowledge I received, or I will just listen to whatever is on their heart. If nothing comes of it, no sweat. Just stay sensitive. You might develop your own style of approaching people. Different approaches work in different situations. There is no one way to do it, so feel free to experiment. It is important, though, to be sensitive to the person. Don't pressure them, and don't be weirder than necessary. Make it your goal to help that person feel loved throughout the encounter.

Conclusion

GOD IS FUN. BOREDOM IN YOUR CHRISTIAN WALK CAN only be symptomatic of either ignorance or disobedience. God is looking for people who are in love with Him, who will walk in their identity as God's kids, united with Christ and united on His mission. He is looking for people who have his heart and will say yes to Him. Will you say yes?

There are people all around you who are desperate for a miracle, in need of a word from the Father, and who need to hear the gospel of Jesus Christ. God is looking for people who will be His healing hands to a hurting world. He is looking for people who will speak His message of reconciliation to a world that is estranged from

Him. He longs to be the Father to an orphan world. He longs to love on those who hate Him. He longs to rescue those who are bound in darkness and oppressed by the power of the enemy.

Understand who you really are! You are the temple of the Holy Spirit. You are one flesh with Christ and united with Him in spirit. You are seated with Him in the heavenly realms at the right hand of the Father. You are Christ's representatives on the earth. You are the light of the world. It is time to shine. It is time to say yes to Him and begin the adventurous life of yielding to the Holy Spirit.

May the God who is never changing, never failing, always faithful, always true, able to heal and deliver, and able to empower you with His precious Holy Spirit be with you. May He guide you with His voice. May you learn to say what He says and do what He does. May the word of Christ dwell within you richly, bearing fruit of eternal life for you and for the world around you. May you walk with boldness and courage in the adventure He has waiting for you. And may you learn to say yes to Jesus and no to self.

About the Author

JONMARK BAKER IS A THIRD GENERATION PASTOR. When he was seven-years-old, a move of God swept through his home church, and his life was forever marked with a passion for revival. As a teenager he pursued God for gifts of healing and prophecy and began using them regularly in evangelism.

As a student at Lake Superior State University, JonMark pioneered a campus ministry (Chi Alpha) and served as a campus minister for a total of eight years. In 2019, JonMark joined the pastoral team at Roots Church in Romulus, Michigan, where he now serves as the Spiritual Life Director.

In addition to serving at Roots Church, JonMark travels as an evangelist, holding revival and healing services around the world. He has a passion for equipping the Bride of Christ to step into her true identity and walk in the power of the Holy Spirit in order to shake the world for Jesus.

JonMark lives in the metro Detroit area with his wife, Kara, and son, Evan.

Additional Resources:

For learning to minister healing:

- ➤ *Paid in Full* (DVD movie, including interview with JonMark Baker)

- ➤ *Paid in Full 40-Day Healing Ministry Activation Manual* (book)

- ➤ *Paid in Full* 8-Week Small Group DVD and Curriculum (DVD and PDF download)

For learning to minister prophetically:

- ➤ *Voice of God* (DVD movie, including interview and street ministry footage of JonMark Baker)

- ➤ *Voice of God 40-Day Hearing God Activation Manual* (book)

**All materials are available at
www.SupernaturalTruth.com**

There are also plenty of **free videos, articles, and audio sermons** under the "Free Media" tab at www.SupernaturalTruth.com.